Cambridge English

Objective
Key
for Schools

Practice Test Booklet
without answers

Annette Capel   Wendy Sharp

CAMBRIDGE UNIVERSITY PRESS
Cambridge, New York, Melbourne, Madrid, Cape Town,
Singapore, São Paulo, Delhi, Mexico City

Cambridge University Press
The Edinburgh Building, Cambridge CB2 8RU, UK

www.cambridge.org
Information on this title: www.cambridge.org/9781107658226

© Cambridge University Press 2013

This publication is in copyright. Subject to statutory exception
and to the provisions of relevant collective licensing agreements,
no reproduction of any part may take place without the written
permission of Cambridge University Press.

First published 2009

Printed in Italy by L.E.G.O. S.p.A.

A catalogue record for this publication is available from the British Library

ISBN 978-1-107-62724-6 Student's Book with Answers with CD-ROM
ISBN 978-1-107-66282-7 Student's Book without Answers with CD-ROM
ISBN 978-1-107-64204-1 Teacher's Book with Teacher's Resources Audio CD/CD-ROM
ISBN 978-1-107-69008-0 Class Audio CDs (2)
ISBN 978-1-107-64676-6 Workbook with Answers
ISBN 978-1-107-69921-2 Workbook without Answers
ISBN 978-1-107-66893-5 Student's Book Pack (Student's Book with Answers with CD-ROM and Class Audio CDs (2))
ISBN 978-1-107-60561-9 For Schools Practice Test Booklet with Answers with Audio CD
ISBN 978-1-107-69445-3 For Schools Pack without Answers (Student's Book with CD-ROM and Practice Test Booklet)

Cambridge University Press has no responsibility for the persistence or
accuracy of URLs for external or third-party internet websites referred to in
this publication, and does not guarantee that any content on such websites is,
or will remain, accurate or appropriate. Information regarding prices, travel
timetables and other factual information given in this work is correct at
the time of first printing but Cambridge University Press does not guarantee
the accuracy of such information thereafter.

Contents

Acknowledgements 4

Introduction 5

Test 1   Paper 1   6

           Paper 2   18

           Paper 3   24

**Visual materials for Paper 3
(Tests 1 and 2)**   25

Test 2   Paper 1   30

           Paper 2   42

           Paper 3   48

Acknowledgements

The authors and publishers acknowledge the following sources of photographs and are grateful for the permissions granted.

p. 7: Getty Images/AFP; p. 10: Alamy/Juniors Bildarchiv GmbH; p. 12: Alamy/ClassicStock; p. 31: Shutterstock/Sergey Petrov; p. 36: Getty Images/David Clapp.

Introduction

This booklet contains two complete practice tests for the *Cambridge English: Key for Schools* exam. The tests cover topics and language typically included in the exam and also revise the content of *Objective Key*. Students can use these tests on their own or with a teacher.

Key for Schools has the same format and task types as the *Cambridge English: Key exam*, and the level of the two versions is identical. However, the texts and topics are more appropriate to the experiences and interests of younger candidates.

Cambridge English exams cover Common European Framework of Reference for Languages (CEFR) levels A2 to C2 for general English. *Key and Key for Schools* are at Level A2 of the CEFR.

The following 'Can Do' statements show what language learners at this level are generally able to do.

Typical abilities	Reading and Writing	Listening and Speaking
Overall general ability	CAN understand straightforward information within a known area. CAN complete forms and write short, simple letters or postcards related to personal information.	CAN understand simple questions and instructions. CAN express simple opinions or requirements in a familiar context.
Social and Tourist	CAN understand straightforward information on food, standard menus, road signs and messages on automatic cash machines. CAN complete most forms related to personal information.	CAN understand straightforward directions, provided that these are not lengthy or complex. CAN express likes and dislikes in familiar contexts using simple language.
Work	CAN understand most short reports or manuals of a predictable nature within his/her own area of expertise. CAN write a short, comprehensible note of request to a colleague or a known contact in another company.	CAN understand the general meaning of a presentation made at a conference if the language is simple and backed up by visuals or video. CAN state simple requirements within own job area.
Study	CAN understand the general meaning of a simplified textbook or article, reading very slowly. CAN write a very short, simple narrative or description.	CAN understand basic instructions on class time, dates and room numbers. CAN express simple opinions using expressions such as 'I don't agree'.

Candidates who achieve the top grade of Pass with Distinction in the *Key for Schools* exam are awarded a certificate stating that they demonstrated ability at Level B1.

The *Key for Schools* exam is a basic qualification in English and can also be a first step for those wishing to progress to the *Cambridge English: Preliminary for Schools* at Level B1.

Good luck with these tests, and with *Cambridge English: Key for Schools*!

Test 1

Paper 1 (1 hour 10 minutes)

Reading and Writing Part 1

Questions 1–5

Which notice (**A–H**) says this (**1–5**)?
For questions **1–5**, mark the correct letter **A–H** on your answer sheet.

Example:

0   You can't use this in class.   Answer: 0 [H]

1   If students are learning this instrument, they need to come on a different day.

2   You won't be able to do this sport if you forget this.

3   You cannot eat anything in here.

4   Go to another place for your lesson.

5   These are available to buy now.

A   **No food or drink in computer room**

B   There is no tennis team practice today.

C   *Remember to bring your swimming costume tomorrow*

D   The library will close at 3.00 today

E   Piano lessons are now on Monday lunchtime not Tuesday

F   **Tickets for the school play are on sale at the office**

G   Room change – Mrs Moon's History class in room 5 this afternoon

H   **Turn your mobile off during lessons**

Reading and Writing Part 2

Questions 6–10

Read the sentences about a holiday.
Choose the best word (**A, B** or **C**) for each space.
For questions **6–10**, mark **A, B** or **C** on your answer sheet.

Example:

0   Last month, Lisa .... sightseeing in India with her aunt and uncle.

   A   went   **B**   made   **C**   took   *Answer:* | 0 | A ■ | B ☐ | C ☐ |

---

6   Lisa .... all her clothes in a large suitcase.

   A   added   **B**   filled   **C**   packed

7   Lisa's uncle had a guidebook with lots of .... information about what to see.

   A   various   **B**   useful   **C**   ready

8   Lisa and her aunt .... a morning shopping in the markets.

   A   spent   **B**   did   **C**   gave

9   There were .... from all over the world staying at Lisa's hotel.

   A   colleagues   **B**   passengers   **C**   guests

10 Lisa .... wanted to ride on an elephant when she was in India.

   A   really   **B**   already   **C**   easily

Test 1

Reading and Writing Part 3

Questions 11–15

Complete the five conversations.
For questions **11–15**, mark **A**, **B** or **C** on your answer sheet.

Example:

11	Would you like to come to my birthday party?	A	I don't agree!
		B	I've had some!
		C	I'd love to!

12	Shall we go to the swimming pool after school?	A	That's all right.
		B	If you like.
		C	See you soon.

13	I've had a bad cold.	A	Poor you!
		B	How do you do?
		C	We did it.

14	Who does that pen belong to?	A	I have that.
		B	I'm sure.
		C	I think it's mine.

15	The café didn't have any burgers.	A	That's a pity.
		B	It isn't here.
		C	There it is.

8

Questions 16–20

Complete the telephone conversation between two friends.
What does Adriana say to Nina?
For questions **16–20**, mark the correct letter **A–H** on your answer sheet.

Example:

Nina: Hi, Adriana. It's Nina.

Adriana: 0 ...D...   Answer: | 0 | A ☐ B ☐ C ☐ D ■ E ☐ F ☐ G ☐ H ☐ |

Nina: Great. I'm ringing about the after-school clubs.

Adriana: 16 ....

Nina: There's a computer club twice a week.

Adriana: 17 ....

Nina: OK, well we could try the dance class. That's only on Mondays.

Adriana: 18 ....

Nina: I don't think so. We can wear our trainers to dance in.

Adriana: 19 ....

Nina: Lucky you! Where did you get them?

Adriana: 20 ....

Nina: OK, see you tomorrow then!

A   I went there with her last week.

B   That sounds better. Is it expensive?

C   Great – I've just got a new pair.

D   Hi. How are you?

E   I really like them.

F   Oh, yes. Did you find out anything about them?

G   My mum got them for me online.

H   That's a lot.

Test 1

Reading and Writing Part 4

Questions 21–27

Read the article about looking after monkeys.
Are sentences **21–27** 'Right' **(A)** or 'Wrong' **(B)**?
If there is not enough information to answer 'Right' **(A)** or 'Wrong' **(B)**, choose 'Doesn't say' **(C)**.
For questions **21–27**, mark **A**, **B** or **C** on your answer sheet.

Animal Park

My name is Dr Carla Conran and, together with my husband, I first opened Animal Park, a special park for chimpanzees, 30 years ago. There are now over 60 of these animals here. People bring chimpanzees to us which need looking after – they are sometimes ill or not wanted by a zoo or are too difficult to keep as pets.

Chimpanzees are very intelligent and they can understand what other chimpanzees, and also people, are feeling. They are very good with their hands and they often use bits of wood to get insects out of trees to eat. The chimpanzees enjoy eating many different kinds of things. It is important to keep the chimpanzees interested, so the staff put the their food in different places every day so they have to find it. The staff also play lots of games with them.

The chimpanzees in our park live in groups of about ten and they become good friends with the others in their group. One group is called Sally's group. Sally likes adventure. Most chimpanzees don't like getting wet but Sally loves it and goes into the pool to swim in the summer.

Paper 1: Reading and Writing

Example:

0   Dr Carla Conran started Animal Park with another person.

   A   Right   B   Wrong   C   Doesn't say   *Answer:* 0 [A ■] [B ☐] [C ☐]

---

21   More than 60 chimpanzees live at the park.

   A   Right   B   Wrong   C   Doesn't say

22   Some of the chimpanzees were sick when they came to the park.

   A   Right   B   Wrong   C   Doesn't say

23   Dr Conran thinks that chimpanzees are better at using their hands than many animals.

   A   Right   B   Wrong   C   Doesn't say

24   The chimpanzees at the park prefer one type of food.

   A   Right   B   Wrong   C   Doesn't say

25   The staff think the chimpanzees should always know where their food will be.

   A   Right   B   Wrong   C   Doesn't say

26   Sally came to the park with a group of chimpanzees.

   A   Right   B   Wrong   C   Doesn't say

27   Sally enjoys doing something unusual for animals of her type.

   A   Right   B   Wrong   C   Doesn't say

Reading and Writing Part 5

Questions 28–35

Read the article about bad weather.
Choose the best word (**A, B** or **C**) for each space.
For questions **28–35**, mark **A, B** or **C** on your answer sheet.

Wind and storms

The world's windiest place is **(0)** .... Antarctica, where there are 95 kph (kilometres per hour) winds **(28)** .... five months of the year. In 1806, a man called Sir Francis Beaufort gave different types of wind a number from 1 to 12. Number 10, **(29)** .... a wind is between 89 and 102 kph, is called a storm. A hurricane is the type of wind **(30)** .... is number 12.

Hurricanes **(31)** .... be very dangerous over a large area and there will often be a lot of rain **(32)** .... a hurricane. Hurricanes **(33)** .... over the sea. Hurricane Katrina was one of the worst hurricanes in the USA and after Katrina finished **(34)** .... people had no homes.

However, wind is also useful. In some countries, **(35)** .... is used to make electricity.

Example:

0	A	in	B	on	C	at	Answer: 0 A ■ B ☐ C ☐

28	A	since	B	between	C	for
29	A	as	B	when	C	because
30	A	who	B	why	C	which
31	A	can	B	need	C	has
32	A	about	B	during	C	to
33	A	begin	B	begins	C	beginning
34	A	much	B	every	C	many
35	A	it	B	there	C	those

Test 1

Reading and Writing Part 6

Questions 36–40

Read the descriptions of some words for things you can find in a flat.
What is the word for each one?
The first letter is already there. There is one space for each other letter in the word.
For questions **36–40**, write the words on your answer sheet.

Example:

0   You can sit at this when you study.   **d _ _ _**

Answer: | **0** | desk |

---

36   You can put some of your clothes in these.   **d _ _ _ _ _ _**

37   You can have a shower and clean your teeth in here.   **b _ _ _ _ _ _ _**

38   You can sit on this with your friends to watch TV or read a book.   **s _ _ _**

39   If you look through these, you can see what is happening outside.   **w _ _ _ _ _ _**

40   This is sometimes made of wood or glass, and people often put
         fruit in it.   **b _ _ _**

Reading and Writing Part 7

Questions 41–50

Complete the message left on the internet by a boy from Spain.
Write ONE word for each space.
For questions **41–50**, write the words on your answer sheet.

Example: | **0** | is |

My name **(0)** .... Alejandro Barrero. I'm twelve years old. My hobby is playing computer games. I got an expensive computer **(41)** .... my birthday and I spend a **(42)** .... of time playing on it.

I think **(43)** .... best game in the world is *Fun Taxi*. You pick **(44)** .... passengers and take them **(45)** .... they want to go as quickly as possible. *Fun Taxi* is better **(46)** .... many other games because you have to drive very fast. You can even play with a friend, against **(47)** .... other! The game **(48)** .... really good music on it and it isn't difficult **(49)** .... play. It doesn't cost very **(50)** .... money if you buy it online.

Test 1

Reading and Writing Part 8

Questions 51–55

Read the notice and the email.
Fill in the information in Antonio's notes.
For questions **51–55**, write the information on your answer sheet.

Football training after school

Classes with Mr Black or Mr Hill

Wednesdays 4–5 p.m. or
Fridays 6–7 p.m.

Remember to bring kit

£5 per lesson or £40 for the term

From: Antonio
To: Pietro

Football training looks good. Shall we do the course with Mr Hill? The later time is better for me. It's cheaper for the whole term – will that be OK? I'll ask my parents for some boots as mine are too small. Shall we meet at 5.30 because it starts at 6.00?

Antonio

Antonio's notes

Class:	Football training
Day	**51**
Teacher:	**52** Mr
New kit needed:	**53**
Need to pay:	**54** £
Time to meet Pietro:	**55**

16

Reading and Writing Part 9

Question 56

You are going to the zoo next Saturday with your English friend, Sam.
Write an email to Sam.

Tell Sam:

- **what time** to meet

- **where** to meet

- **what** to bring.

Write **25–35** words.

Write the email on your answer sheet.

Test 1

Paper 2 (approximately 30 minutes including 8 minutes' transfer time)

Listening Part 1

Questions 1–5

You will hear five short conversations.
You will hear each conversation twice.
There is one question for each conversation.
For each question, choose the right answer (**A**, **B** or **C**).

Example: How many people belong to the swimming club?

A 8   B 15 (circled)   C 30

---

1 Where will Susie and Franco do their homework?

A

B

C

2 What is Ben going to buy for his mother's birthday?

A

B

C

18

Paper 2: Listening

3 What did Josie like best about the TV cooking programme?

A B C

4 What has Katie broken?

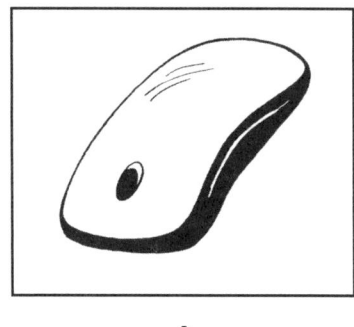  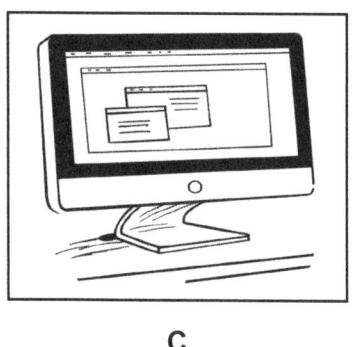

A B C

5 What time will the theme park close next Saturday?

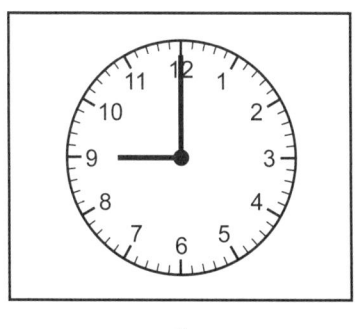 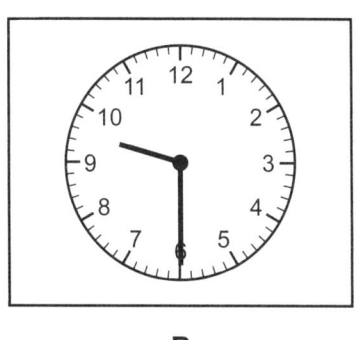 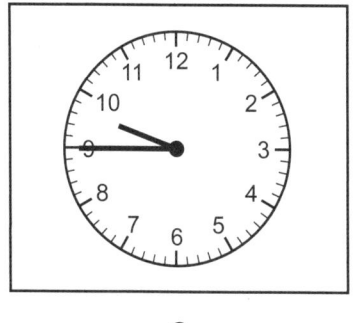

A B C

Test 1

Listening Part 2

Questions 6–10

Listen to Sam telling his sister about his friends' favourite food.
Which food does each person prefer?
For questions **6–10**, write a letter **A–H** next to each person.
You will hear the conversation twice.

Example:

0   Paul | E |

PEOPLE		FOOD
6 Mark		A burgers
		B cake
7 Sergio		
		C chocolate
8 Jenny		D fruit
		E ice cream
9 Lisa		
		F pasta
10 Ben		G pizza
		H salad

20

Listening Part 3

Questions 11–15

Listen to Rebecca talking to a friend about a school art show.
For each question, choose the right answer (**A**, **B** or **C**).
You will hear the conversation twice.

Example:

0   Which day does the art show start?

   (A)   Tuesday

   B   Thursday

   C   Saturday

---

11   Where can you see the pictures?

   A   in the school hall

   B   in the sports hall

   C   in the classrooms

12   Which picture does Rebecca have in the art show?

   A   a person

   B   a building

   C   a mountain

13   Who is opening the art show?

   A   the headteacher

   B   an actor

   C   a singer

14   What is Rebecca doing at the art show?

   A   selling tickets

   B   serving drinks

   C   talking to visitors

15   What time will the art show close each day?

   A   4.30

   B   5.30

   C   6.30

Test 1

Listening Part 4

Questions 16–20

You will hear a girl, Miriam, asking a friend about a museum.
Listen and complete each question.
You will hear the conversation twice.

Hendry Museum

Museum is in:	London
Cost for a family:	(16) £ ....
Name of nearest underground station:	(17) ....
Best floor of museum to visit:	(18) ....
Opening time:	(19) ....
Cheap thing(s) to buy:	(20) ....

Paper 2: Listening

Listening Part 5

Questions 21–25

You will hear a teacher telling his class about a geography project.
Listen and complete each question.
You will hear the information twice.

Geography project

Subject of project:	Tallworth Old Bridge
Year built:	**(21)** ....
Bridge paid for by:	**(22)** a ....

Visit to bridge

Cost of museum:	**(23)** £ ....
Remember to bring:	**(24)** a ....
Date of visit:	**(25)** ....

23

Test 1

Paper 3

About the Speaking test

Part 1 (5–6 minutes)

In this part, the examiner asks you questions to find out personal information, such as your surname, where you are from, where you live and about your family. You may also need to answer questions about your daily life, for example your school or hobbies.

Part 2 (3–4 minutes)

In this part, you and your partner(s) talk together. You ask and answer questions to find out information. The examiner will give you a card with some information on it. The examiner will give your partner another card with some words to help them make questions. Your partner will ask you questions, and you need to read the information on your card to answer the questions. You will then change roles with your partner.

Visual materials for Paper 3

Tests 1 and 2

Visual materials

1A

New play

Come and see our young actors on stage in

'The Forest'
by Thomas Maxwell

at Oakwood School Theatre
Saturday 10 July
7.30 – 10.30 pm

Tickets: £15 adults,
£8 children under 12,
£6 students

1C

School visit to Longhill farm – £12

See lots of cows, chickens and sheep and horses.

Thursday 21 November
(bus leaves 8.30, return
to school for 4.30)

Bring notebook and pen

Café at farm

1B

School play

- name / play?
- date / play?
- where / play?
- how much /students?
- what time / finish?

1D

Farm visit

- date / visit?
- which / animals?
- how / travel?
- what / bring?
- where / eat?

2A

Sports day
Thursday 14 July
2.30 – 4.45 pm

100-metre races, football, volleyball

T-shirts for winners!

Cake and ice cream for sale - only £1.50

2C

School magazine

COMING NEXT MONTH!

New school magazine called KIDS

16 pages, all in colour

Articles on music and sports

Interested in writing something? – Tell Dani in Class 4B

2B

Sports day

- which / sports?
- what / prizes?
- food?
- date / sports day?
- when / start?

2D

School magazine

- name / magazine?
- when / available?
- who / contact?
- what / articles?
- number / pages?

Test 2

Paper 1 (1 hour 10 minutes)

Reading and Writing Part 1

Questions 1–5

Which notice (**A–H**) says this (**1–5**)?
For questions **1–5**, mark the correct letter **A–H** on your answer sheet.

Example:

0   You can only use a camera outside.   Answer: 0 A☐ B☐ C☐ D■ E☐ F☐ G☐ H☐

1   If you are with lots of people, use another entrance.

2   In bad weather, make sure you walk up to the castle slowly.

3   Some things for children cost less than usual at the moment.

4   You can still have a meal at the castle, but in a different place.

5   It is possible to join a group to visit the castle this afternoon.

A   TAKE GREAT CARE OUTSIDE IF CASTLE PATH IS WET!

B   Castle Restaurant closed today but café is serving lunches until 3pm

C   Sorry, the 11.00 tour is fully booked – next one starts at 2.30

D   NO PHOTOS INSIDE THE CASTLE – POSTCARDS FOR SALE IN SHOP

E   All groups should enter the castle through the west door – not here

F   Children must be careful when walking past the castle furniture

G   Models, toys and games all **half-price** this week
(Shop open until 5 pm)

H   Ticket prices for visitors:
Adults £8.00
Under 16s £5.00   Under 5s free

Paper 1: Reading and Writing

Reading and Writing Part 2

Questions 6–10

Read the sentences about a special school visitor.
Choose the best word (**A, B** or **C**) for each space.
For questions **6–10**, mark **A, B** or **C** on your answer sheet.

Example:

0   The famous dancer Helena Murray .... to her old school yesterday.

   A   went   **B**   entered   **C**   arrived   *Answer:* | 0 | A ■ | B ☐ | C ☐ |

---

6   Helena .... to the children in the school hall.

   A   said   **B**   told   **C**   spoke

7   The children had .... to ask Helena about her work.

   A   area   **B**   time   **C**   place

8   Helena was .... to answer all their questions.

   A   excellent   **B**   happy   **C**   pleasant

9   Helena was taken on a tour of the school ....

   A   afterwards   **B**   once   **C**   nearly

10   The school was much .... than she remembered.

   A   taller   **B**   wider   **C**   bigger

Test 2

Reading and Writing Part 3

Questions 11–15

Complete the five conversations.
For questions **11–15**, mark **A**, **B** or **C** on your answer sheet.

Example:

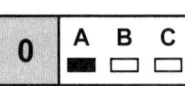

---

11 How much homework have you got for tonight?
   A I've got it now.
   B There is a lot sometimes.
   C Less than yesterday.

12 I'm going climbing with my brother this weekend.
   A It's mine.
   B Be careful!
   C Of course not.

13 Why not come to the cinema with us?
   A Who's coming instead?
   B Which film did you see?
   C When are you planning to go?

14 Can you help me with this maths problem?
   A If you like.
   B Well done!
   C Don't forget.

15 I'm sorry I'm late for class.
   A What time do you start?
   B What happened?
   C What day?

Questions 16–20

Complete the conversation between two friends.
What does Eva say to Jane?
For questions **16–20**, mark the correct letter **A–H** on your answer sheet.

Example:

Jane: Hi, Eva. Can I ask you about our science project?

Eva: 0 ..B.......   Answer:

Jane: What date do we have to finish it by?

Eva: **16** ....

Jane: I hope so! I've got lots of other homework.

Eva: **17** ....

Jane: Good idea. How about working on it together here?

Eva: **18** ....

Jane: Lucky you! Let's do it the next day, then.

Eva: **19** ....

Jane: Let's use Dad's computer. It's really fast.

Eva: **20** ....

Jane: Perfect. See you then.

A And it's got a bigger screen. Is 10 o'clock OK?

B Sure. What do you need to know?

C Great, but not on Saturday because I'm at the beach.

D I'll have hockey practice that afternoon as well.

E Me too. That's why I'm planning to do mine at the weekend.

F Thanks, Sunday's fine. Shall I bring my laptop?

G We can find most of the information online instead.

H Next Tuesday. Will that give you enough time?

Test 2

Reading and Writing Part 4

Questions 21–27

Read the article about three young sports players in Britain and then answer the questions. For questions **21–27**, mark **A**, **B** or **C** on your answer sheet.

LIAM

I started playing badminton for fun in the garden with my sisters when I was four. Then I had tennis lessons and forgot all about badminton until I was 11. I changed schools then and my new sports teacher got me interested again. I've already won two national competitions in my age group and I came third in an international one in Holland last month. I've just added another eight hours to my competition training timetable so I might win next time!

ADE

We only play football at school and I wanted to try another kind of sport, so I looked online for information. I found a hockey club near my home and they've been fantastic. My dad was on the university hockey team and is still at that level, so he helps me too. I'd like to improve and play more matches, but I'll never be good enough for the national team.

JOSEPH

Last year I entered table tennis competitions in France and Spain, but I didn't win anything. I've hurt my arm so I'm having a break from playing at the moment. That means I need to keep fit by running instead. My dream is to be in our national team when I'm older. Nobody in my family has ever played table tennis, but my parents and uncle are fans now and they follow it on the internet.

Example:

0   Who played his sport at home when he was younger?

    A   Liam   **B**   Ade   **C**   Joseph   *Answer:* **0** A■ B☐ C☐

---

21   Who has a parent that plays the same sport?

    A   Liam   **B**   Ade   **C**   Joseph

22   Who needs to take another kind of exercise at the moment?

    A   Liam   **B**   Ade   **C**   Joseph

23   Who has done well in a competition abroad?

    A   Liam   **B**   Ade   **C**   Joseph

24   Who had a break of several years from playing his sport?

    A   Liam   **B**   Ade   **C**   Joseph

25   Who had to find out more about his sport on the internet?

    A   Liam   **B**   Ade   **C**   Joseph

26   Who hopes to get good enough to play for his country?

    A   Liam   **B**   Ade   **C**   Joseph

27   Who spends longer practising before matches now?

    A   Liam   **B**   Ade   **C**   Joseph

Test 2

Reading and Writing Part 5

Questions 28–35

Read the article about 'manga', Japanese comics.
Choose the best word (**A, B** or **C**) for each space.
For questions **28–35**, mark **A**, **B** or **C** on your answer sheet.

Manga

Manga is the Japanese word **(0)** .... comics or cartoons. In Japan, people of all ages read these stories and there are **(28)** .... special cafés where people drink coffee and read manga. **(29)** .... kinds of manga are available, **(30)** .... adventure, love stories and so on. The manga books and magazines that are read **(31)** .... Japanese boys look very different from **(32)** .... written for Japanese girls.

Sales of manga have grown a lot in Japan **(33)** .... the 1950s. Most Japanese manga is **(34)** .... just in black and white. Some international manga comics are **(35)** .... this too, but colour ones are usually more popular.

Paper 1: Reading and Writing

Example:

| 0 | A | for | B | to | C | with | Answer: | 0 | A ■ | B ☐ | C ☐ |

| 28 | A | instead | B | almost | C | even |

| 29 | A | Many | B | Every | C | Much |

| 30 | A | included | B | includes | C | including |

| 31 | A | of | B | by | C | at |

| 32 | A | these | B | them | C | those |

| 33 | A | since | B | until | C | between |

| 34 | A | already | B | yet | C | still |

| 35 | A | as | B | like | C | than |

37

Test 2

Reading and Writing Part 6

Questions 36–40

Read the descriptions of some words for things you might take on a picnic.
What is the word for each one?
The first letter is already there. There is one space for each other letter in the word.
For questions **36–40**, write the words on your answer sheet.

Example:

0   This is often made of wool and you can sit on it during your picnic.   b _ _ _ _ _ _

Answer:	0	blanket

36   You will need these to drink coffee from.   c _ _ _

37   Bananas, apples and oranges are all examples of this.   f _ _ _ _ _

38   This has two slices of bread with cold food like meat or cheese in the middle.   s _ _ _ _ _ _ _

39   You need this to cut a large cake into small pieces.   k _ _ _ _

40   After your picnic, you can kick this around on the grass with your friends.   f _ _ _ _ _ _ _

Reading and Writing Part 7

Questions 41–50

Complete this email.
Write ONE word for each space.
For questions **41–50**, write the words on your answer sheet.

Example: | **0** | what |

Hi Julia

Guess **(0)** ....? I'm doing a great course on cookery **(41)** .... the moment. There **(42)** .... ten lessons and the course is **(43)** .... Saturday mornings. The teacher is really nice and I'm learning lots **(44)** .... different things. Last week we made pizzas and we ate **(45)** .... after the lesson. We **(46)** .... asked by the teacher to choose the best one, which was fun. My pizza didn't win, **(47)** .... I didn't mind.

How **(48)** .... cooking do you do? Tell **(49)** .... about your favourite meal. **(50)** .... is the pasta with chilli sauce that my mum makes!

Love

Tomas

Test 2

Reading and Writing Part 8

Questions 51–55

Read the poster and the email to Sam.
Fill in the information in Sam's notes.
For questions **51–55**, write the information on your answer sheet.

SONG COMPETITION

Write and record a song and win a guitar!

Songs can be about anything you choose

Two age groups:
11–15 win a guitar
16–18 win a keyboard

Send in your songs by June 30 – only £4.00 per song

From: Jo
To: Sam

Hi Sam

I just saw this poster. It's perfect for 13-year-olds like us. We've written some great songs – let's send them 'Beach' – it's better than 'Crying'. We can practise on Tuesday and record it together at school on Wednesday. Shall we pay half each? I'll give you £2.00 tomorrow.

Jo

Sam's notes
Competition

Last date to enter competition:	June 30
Name of our song:	**51**
Cost for one song in competition:	**52** £
Our age group:	**53**
Prize:	**54**
Day to record song with Jo:	**55**

40

Paper 1: Reading and Writing

Reading and Writing Part 9

Question 56

Read the email from your English friend, Alex.

>
>
> I saw a great film yesterday. What is the best film you've seen this year? What is it about? Why did you like it?

Write an email to Alex and answer the questions.
Write **25–35** words.
Write the email on your answer sheet.

Test 2

Paper 2 (approximately 30 minutes including 8 minutes' transfer time)

Listening Part 1

Questions 1–5

You will hear five short conversations.
You will hear each conversation twice.
There is one question for each conversation.
For each question, choose the right answer (**A**, **B** or **C**).

Example: How many people belong to the swimming club?

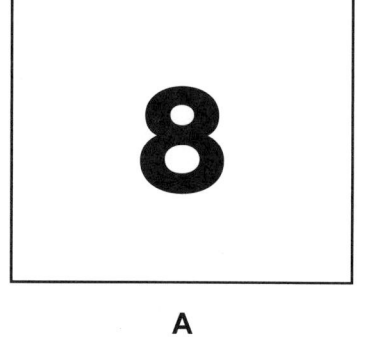

A    B   C

---

1   How did the boy get back from his football match?

A   B   C

2   Which date is Ben's birthday?

A   B   C

Paper 2: Listening

3 What is Anna going to do after school today?

A

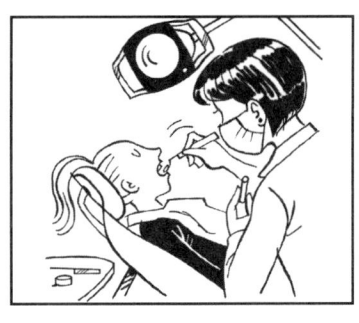

B

C

4 Which is Jenny's project folder?

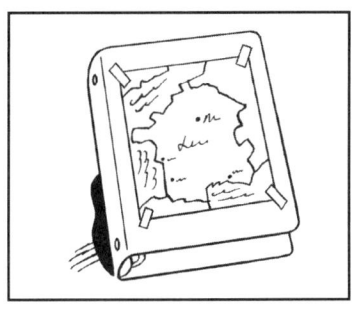

A

B

C

5 Where will the friends meet?

A

B

C

Test 2

Listening Part 2

Questions 6–10

Listen to Maria telling a friend about the activities she did on a course last week.
What activity did she do on each day?
For questions **6–10**, write a letter **A–H** next to each day.
You will hear the conversation twice.

Example:

0   Monday   A

	DAYS			ACTIVITIES
6	Tuesday		A	basketball
			B	climbing
7	Wednesday			
			C	cycling
8	Thursday		D	horse riding
			E	running
9	Friday			
			F	sailing
10	Saturday		G	swimming
			H	tennis

44

Listening Part 3

Questions 11–15

Listen to Max telling a friend about a writing competition for students.
For each question, choose the right answer (**A**, **B** or **C**).
You will hear the conversation twice.

Example:

0   The competition is for students no older than

  A   10.

  B   11.

  (C)   14.

---

11   For this year's competition, students must write a story about

  A   the sea.

  B   an old man.

  C   a castle.

12   Which month does the competition end?

  A   January

  B   February

  C   March

13   What is the first prize?

  A   a camera

  B   a phone

  C   a laptop

14   Who will choose the winning stories?

  A   a footballer

  B   a journalist

  C   a famous writer

15   Students entering their stories should

  A   send them by post.

  B   email them with a form.

  C   take them to the office.

Test 2

Listening Part 4

Questions 16–20

You will hear a girl, Karen, phoning a bookshop about a dictionary.
Listen and complete each question.
You will hear the conversation twice.

Dictionary for Sale

Name of bookshop: English Centre

Number of pages in bigger dictionary: (16) ....

Price of dictionary this week: (17) $ ....

Shop is next to: (18) ....

Time shop closes on weekdays: (19) .... p.m.

Free gift: (20) ....

Paper 2: Listening

Listening Part 5

Questions 21–25

You will hear a science teacher telling her students about a day trip.
Listen and complete each question.
You will hear the information twice.

Science Trip

Date: September 28th

Don't forget to wear: (21) ....

Coach journey will take: (22) .... minutes

Study centre film is about: (23) ....

Number of students per group: (24) ....

Name of new science teacher: (25) Mrs ....

Test 2

Paper 3

About the Speaking test

Part 1 (5–6 minutes)

In this part, the examiner asks you questions to find out personal information, such as your surname, where you are from, where you live and about your family. You may also need to answer questions about your daily life, for example your school or hobbies.

Part 2 (3–4 minutes)

In this part, you and your partner(s) talk together. You ask and answer questions to find out information. The examiner will give you a card with some information on it. The examiner will give your partner another card with some words to help them make questions. Your partner will ask you questions, and you need to read the information on your card to answer the questions. You will then change roles with your partner.

Grammar First conditional

- Find the sentence in the text which begins with *If* ...
  If ....
- Which tenses are used?
  If + ...
- We use this structure to express a possible condition.

3 Match the sentence beginnings 1–6 with their endings A–F.

1 If I get up 7 o'clock,	A I'll get a good job.
2 If I go swimming every day,	B I'll travel round the world.
	C I'll sleep better at night.
3 If I work hard at school,	D I'll get fit.
4 If I save my money,	E I won't be late for school.
5 If I win the lottery,	F I'll buy a TV for my bedroom.
6 If I drink less coffee,	

- When the sentence begins with *if*, we often use a comma. We can also use *if* in the middle of a sentence without a comma.

G → page 147

4 We all need enough sleep at night. What other things will make you healthier? Talk to your partner about the things below and add two more ideas of your own.

1 eating burgers
2 riding a motorbike
3 working long hours
4 too much stress
5 having a holiday
6 watching TV all day

EXAMPLE: *If you eat fewer burgers and more vegetables you will feel better.*

5 You are going on a camping holiday in the mountains with a friend. Talk about what you will do if you have problems.

EXAMPLE: A: *What will you do if you have an accident?*
B: *I'll use my mobile phone to ring someone.*

6 Complete the sentences.

If I work harder, I will ...
If I don't ...
If I get up ...
If ...

7 Write a note to a friend about what you are going to do to become healthier. Say:
- why you want to get fit
- what you are going to do
- when or how often you are going to do it.

Write 25–35 words.

Spelling spot
Words which don't double their last letter

The last letter isn't doubled if a word ends in
- two consonants:
  help   helped   helping
- two vowels and a consonant:
  need   needed   needing

8 Are these words correct? Put a tick or a cross beside each one.

1 cheaper
2 fastter
3 getting
4 stoping
5 waiting
6 running
7 thiner
8 swiming

Activity
An interview

For homework interview the oldest person you know – maybe a grandparent or a neighbour or even your parents! Prepare a chart where you can write in the information. Report back to the class what you found out.

Use these words to make questions:

1 when / you / born
2 how / you / keep / healthy
3 what / you / eat
4 what / changes / you / see
5 what / you / think of / internet/

Exam folder 10

Reading Part 4 Multiple choice

In Part 4 of the Reading and Writing paper, there can be different types of task. You will only have to answer one of these in the exam. See Exam folder 6 on page 66 for information about the 'Right, Wrong, Doesn't Say' task.

For the multiple-choice task, you will have to read one long article or three short articles. There are seven questions (**21–27**) and an example at the beginning. Each question has a choice of three answers (**A**, **B** or **C**). You must choose the correct answer.

Part 4			
21	A	B	C
22	A	B	C
23	A	B	C
24	A	B	C
25	A	B	C
26	A	B	C
27	A	B	C

One long article

1 Read the instructions and the article about John Flynn quickly.
   What is it about?

   A An Australian sheep farmer.
   B A British doctor living in Australia.
   C An Australian who had a new idea.

2 Now do the exam task, following the advice.

EXAM ADVICE

- Read the instructions to find out what the article is about.
- Read the whole article quickly before you answer any of the questions.
- Don't worry if there is a word you don't understand.
- Read each question very carefully. The questions are in the order in which you will find the answers in the article.
- Underline the place in the article where you find each answer.
- Decide on the correct answer (A, B or C).
- Look at the article to check that the other choices are wrong.
- Mark your answers on your answer sheet. There is an example of the answer sheet for Part 4 above.

Part 4

Questions 21–27

Read the article about a famous Australian man, called John Flynn.

For questions **21–27**, mark **A**, **B** or **C** on your answer sheet.

The Flying Doctor

John Flynn was born in Australia in 1880. His father was a schoolteacher. John studied hard and in 1911 he left the city of Melbourne and went to work in South Australia for a church. The church wanted to help the sheep farmers who lived in the outback – the countryside area many kilometres from towns and cities. They built a number of small hospitals and found nurses to work in them. But at that time there were only two doctors in all of South Australia.

One story Flynn often told was of Jimmy Darcy. One day Jimmy had an accident on his farm so friends took him to see F.W. Tuckett, who worked at the post office at Halls Creek. It was a journey of 22 km. Tuckett was the only person in the area who knew anything about medicine. He wanted to help but Jimmy was too ill. Tuckett finally talked by radio to a doctor in Perth, a city 1500 km away. The doctor took ten days to arrive. He travelled by car, by horse and on foot and when he arrived, he found that Jimmy was already dead.

Flynn saw that planes could really help people in the outback. He wrote about his idea for a 'Flying Doctor' in 1917 but it wasn't until 1928 that one actually took off. By the 1930s there was a Flying Doctor plane in every part of Australia.

Example:

0   John Flynn's job was   A teaching at a school.
                           B helping with sheep farming.
                           C working for the church.   Answer:

21 Flynn worked in   A a city.
                                                 B the countryside.
                                                 C a small town.

22 What was the problem in South Australia?   A The nurses weren't very good.
                                                 B There were no hospitals.
                                                 C There weren't enough doctors.

23 What does Flynn tell us about Jimmy?   A He lived at Halls Creek.
                                                 B He was a farmer.
                                                 C He was often ill.

24 Why did Jimmy and his friends go to see   A He helped sick people.
    F.W. Tuckett?   B He worked at a post office.
                                                 C He was a doctor.

25 What did F.W. Tuckett decide to do?   A to give Jimmy some medicine
                                                 B to go with Jimmy to the city
                                                 C to use a radio to get help for Jimmy

26 What do we know about the doctor from Perth? A He travelled too slowly to save Jimmy.
                                                 B He had problems with his car.
                                                 C He didn't know the way to Halls Creek.

27 The first Flying Doctor plane flew in   A 1917.
                                                 B 1928.
                                                 C 1930.

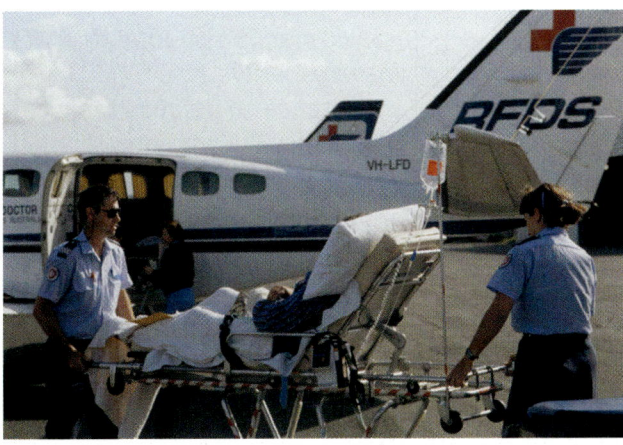

Turn over.

There is another Part 4 exam task on the next page.

EXAM FOLDER 10   115

Reading Part 4 Multiple choice
Three short articles

EXAM ADVICE

- Read the instructions to find out what the articles are about.
- Read all three articles quickly before you answer any of the questions.
- Don't worry if you don't understand every word.
- Read each question carefully and underline the important words.
- Find the information in the articles that matches these words.
- Decide which article gives the correct answer (A, B or C).
- Underline the part of the article where you found the answer.
- Remember that there will be some 'distraction' in the other articles – for example, another article will use some of the words from the question.
- Check your answers by reading the parts you underlined in the articles.
- Mark your answers on your answer sheet.

Part 4

Questions 21–27

Read the articles about three teenagers and their smartphones and then answer the questions.

For questions **21–27**, mark **A**, **B** or **C** on your answer sheet.

LEE	**KIM**	**ALEX**
My cousin gave me this phone last year when she got a new one. It can take great pictures but I don't use it for that. I've downloaded lots of free fun things to play, like chess and different puzzles. I've only ever bought one app, to help me plan my homework and tennis practice. My phone's so useful! I can get facts I need for history and geography before my next class.	I lost my last phone when I was sailing – it fell in the sea! This one is only three weeks old and I haven't put any games on it yet. I don't buy many apps and there's only one that I use often. I've got friends all over the world and we email each other cool photos while we're at parties and concerts. It's really important to talk to them too, so I use free websites for that.	My phone was a present from my parents when I became a teenager. It was the latest model then, but that was two years ago! To begin with I used it just to text and speak to my school friends. Now I go online every day to know what's happening at big football matches and find out about my favourite movie stars. I visit foreign newspaper websites sometimes, to improve the languages I'm studying.

Example:

0 Who has the newest phone?

   A Lee   **B** Kim   **C** Alex   Answer: 0 A **B** C

---

21 Who was given the phone as a birthday gift?

   A Lee   **B** Kim   **C** Alex

22 Who has put several games on their phone?

   A Lee   **B** Kim   **C** Alex

23 Who had an accident with an earlier phone?

   A Lee   **B** Kim   **C** Alex

24 Who uses their phone to find out information about school subjects quickly?

   A Lee   **B** Kim   **C** Alex

25 Who takes pictures on their phone and sends them to friends immediately?

   A Lee   **B** Kim   **C** Alex

26 Who uses their phone to check on the latest sports information?

   A Lee   **B** Kim   **C** Alex

27 Who chats to friends in other countries without having to pay anything?

   A Lee   **B** Kim   **C** Alex

19.1 Let's communicate!

Vocabulary

1 Find fifteen words to do with communicating in the word square (look → and ↓). Use the pictures to help you. One has been done for you.

c	a	l	l	r	o	m	a	y	i
w	e	n	v	e	l	o	p	e	n
i	t	f	a	c	e	b	o	o	k
n	s	u	f	e	a	i	s	r	n
t	e	x	t	i	l	l	t	i	o
e	n	e	e	v	l	e	c	n	t
r	d	b	m	e	s	s	a	g	e
n	c	k	a	t	o	m	r	i	t
e	w	r	i	t	e	n	d	a	l
t	t	e	l	e	p	h	o	n	e

Key words → page 152

2 Which ways of communicating are best in these situations? Decide on your answers. Then talk to another student about them, using words from the word square.

1 Your friend in Australia has a birthday in a couple of days, so it's too late to post anything.
2 You've heard that your cousin in another town is getting married.
3 You can't meet your friends tonight and want to say sorry.
4 You want to tell your family where you'll be this evening but no one is at home.
5 You're on holiday and want to show your brother what the place is like.
6 A friend who lives near you has just had some bad news.

Listening

3 🔊 28 Listen to Paul telling a friend how he has communicated some good news. Which way of communicating has he used for each person?

For questions 1–5, write a letter (A–H) next to each person.

EXAMPLE: 0   Ruth   **B**

People
1 Mario
2 Anna
3 Jack
4 Tessa
5 Paul's professor

Ways of communicating
A email
B Facebook
C letter
D mobile phone call
E note
F phone message
G postcard
H text message

UNIT 19 LANGUAGE AND COMMUNICATION

Pronunciation

4 🔊29 Listen again to the parts of the recording below. On the words which are broken into syllables, put a star above the stressed syllable.

1 Con|gra|tu|la*|tions on get*|ting the job!
2 Mario's tra|vel|ling up to Scot|land to|day.
3 I spoke to him on his mo|bile in|stead.
4 I left a mess|age on her phone.
5 Yes, in Ar|gen|ti|na.
6 Re|mem|ber to phone your pro|fess|or and tell him.
7 The num|ber at the u|ni|ver|si|ty has changed.
8 I bought one of that Mo|rocc|an car|pet we saw at the mu|se|um.

Now practise saying the sentences.

Grammar Prepositions of place

In the recording, you heard several phrases with prepositions, for example *at the museum*.

5 Complete each phrase with a preposition from the box and add another similar phrase of your own.

| at   in   on |

1 _at_ home   _at work_
2 .... the floor   ....
3 .... Argentina   ....
4 .... New Street   ....
5 .... 25 Broad Street ....
6 .... Madrid   ....
7 .... the bus stop   ....

6 Correct the mistakes that exam candidates made with prepositions. One sentence is correct.

1 You can call me at my cell phone: 22 59 67 81.
2 I'll meet you on the supermarket in West Street.
3 I'm in holiday now in Istanbul.
4 You can stay on my house.
5 The hotel is at the centre of the town.
6 We live on a new house in Magka.
7 On the walls there are some posters.
8 If you are interested in joining the club, find me at room 12.

 page 147

7 Complete this letter. Write ONE word for each space.

Dear Margareta

How are you? I don't write too (1) .... letters, but I'm sending you this one (2) .... I know you like to receive them. I've bought (3) .... beautiful stamps to put (4) .... the envelope, too. (5) .... my country, the post office often sells stamps showing different birds, like (6) .... ones. I think they're great! (7) .... one is your favourite?

If you get a smartphone for your birthday, (8) .... it have a new number? Please let (9) .... know about that. My mum and dad and (10) .... else in the family send you their best wishes.

Love,

Agnes

Spelling spot

Spelling the sound /iː/

- The sound /iː/ is spelled in different ways in English.

beginning	middle	end
email	been	see
easy	mean	tea
	these	we
	police	
	believe	
	ceiling	

8 Fill in the missing vowels.

1 Have you rec_ _ved an email from Jan yet?
2 Here's a fr_ _ pen for you. They cost six euros _ _ch in the shops!
3 Can I sp_ _k to Mrs Lee?
4 What animals are in that f_ _ld over there?
5 I'm going to be away all next w_ _k.
6 I'd like a k_lo of apples.

19.2 Different languages

1. How many languages do you speak? Do you speak a different language or dialect at home? Do your grandparents?

2. Answer this quiz about world languages by saying Right or Wrong. Then discuss your ideas with another student.
   1. Spanish is spoken by more people than any other language.
   2. Japanese is one of the six official languages of the United Nations.
   3. More than 700 languages are spoken in Indonesia.
   4. At least one in three people in Italy speak a dialect as well as Italian.
   5. Cornish and Irish belong to the same language group.

Reading

3. Read this article about the Cornish language. Choose the best word for each space, A, B or C.

0	A ago	B before	C since
1	A This	B Them	C These
2	A on	B in	C at
3	A another	B others	C other
4	A to	B until	C for
5	A more	B much	C many
6	A is	B has	C was
7	A its	B their	C her
8	A bring	B bringing	C brought

The history of Cornish

Around 4000 years (**0**) .... , the group of languages now called the Celtic languages started to develop. (**1**) .... languages then became two different groups. Cornish, Welsh and Breton – the language spoken (**2**) .... north-west France – are one group, and Irish and Scots Gaelic are part of the (**3**) ....

Cornish grew like a modern European language (**4**) .... the 17th century, when English became (**5**) .... important in Cornwall than earlier. English (**6**) .... used to buy and sell things and because of that, Cornish people began to think badly of (**7**) .... language and saw Cornish only as the language of poor people.

By the end of the 19th century, Cornish was no longer spoken. But a man called Henry Jenner studied the language and (**8**) .... it back to life. Now, you can even learn Cornish on the internet!

Grammar Prepositions of time

4 What do you know about prepositions? Fill in the missing prepositions of time: *at, in, on.*

- We use .... with:
  - years 1953
  - centuries .... the 20th century
  - seasons .... (the) summer
  - months .... November
  - parts of the day .... the afternoon

- We use .... with:
  - days of the week .... Saturday
  - special days .... New Year's Day
  - dates .... 1 March 2013

- We use .... with:
  - times .... ten o'clock / 10.00
  - meals .... breakfast
  - festivals .... Easter
  - periods of time .... the weekend

G → page 148

5 Lara studies German and Russian. Ask and answer questions to complete her timetable, using prepositions of time. Student B should turn to page 135 now.

Student A's questions

- Which day … German/Russian Conversation?
- What time?
- When … free?

Do the same for these classes in each language:

Conversation   Grammar
Reading   Writing
Listening

EXAMPLE:
A: *Which day does she have German conversation?*
B: *On Monday.*
A: *What time?*
B: *At three o'clock.*

Vocabulary

6 How many languages do you know the names of? Remember that sometimes the word used for the language is the same word as the nationality. Complete the table.

country	nationality	language(s) spoken
Argentina	Argentinian	
Brazil	Brazilian	
Chile	Chilean	
France	French	
Greece	Greek	
Italy	Italian	
Mexico	Mexican	
Morocco	Moroccan	
Switzerland	Swiss	

Key words → page 152

Activity
What do they speak in …?

- Get into two teams. (And close your books!) Your teacher will give each of you a number.
- When your number is called, say the name of a country. The person with the same number on the opposite team must tell you any one language which is spoken in that country.

  EXAMPLE: Team A person: *Poland*
  Team B person: *Polish*

- Score one point for your team for every language you name correctly.

	Monday	Tuesday	Wednesday	Thursday	Friday
9.00					
10.00					
11.00					
12.00					
1.00			LUNCH		
2.00					
3.00	German Conversation				

UNIT 19 LANGUAGE AND COMMUNICATION

Writing folder 5

Writing Part 9 Short message

In Part 9 (Question **56**) of the Reading and Writing paper, you must write about three different things, using between 25 and 35 words. Sometimes, as in Writing folder 3 (see page 72), you will have to reply to a message from a friend. Sometimes there will just be instructions about what you have to write.

1   Look at these exam answers and decide what three things the candidates were asked to write about. Choose from A–E in the box below.

1
Dear Pat
I'll be free at 10 a.m. We can meet us to Paul's caffe. I'd like to buy a skirt. See you on Saturday.
Love Anya

2
Dear Pat
I will go for two hours. I will meet with John and I will want buy a red bicycle. Your friend

3
Dear Pat I think it is a great idea to go shopping together. We could meet in the bus stop at 12 o'clock in the morning. I'd like to buy some pens. See you soon. Claudia

4
Yes, I coming with you to shopping on Saturday. I'll probably be free at the lunch. We'll meet us to the shopping centre in town. I want to buy me two trousers and a top. Perhaps, I want to buy also a robe. And you, what do you want to buy?
From your best friend
Sylvie

A when you can meet your friend Pat on Saturday
B who you will invite to go shopping with you on Saturday
C where you suggest meeting your friend Pat on Saturday
D what you would like to buy on Saturday
E how you will get to the shopping centre on Saturday

2   Decide which answer is the best and which is the worst. Explain why.

3   Correct any wrong prepositions in the answers and underline other errors.

4   Rewrite answer 4, correcting the errors. Write between 25 and 35 words.

EXAM ADVICE

- Read the question carefully and underline the three things you have to write about.
- Make some quick notes.
- Include an opening formula like *Dear* ... or *Hi* ... with the name.
- Write a rough answer on the question paper first.
- Make sure you write enough words (around 35 is best).
- Use informal English because you are writing to a friend.
- Remember to sign the message with your first name at the end.
- Try to include different nouns and adjectives to show your language range.
- Check grammar, spelling, punctuation and use of capital letters.
- Write your final answer on your answer sheet. Below is an example of the answer sheet for Part 9.

Part 9 (Question 56): Write your answer below.

Part 9

Question 56

You are going to meet your friend Jan at the cinema tomorrow. Write an email to Jan.

Say:

- **when** you will meet at the cinema
- **which film** you want to see
- **why** Jan would enjoy this film.

Write **25–35** words.

Write your email on the answer sheet.

WRITING FOLDER 5

20.1 Famous people

1 Who are these people? Why are they famous? Will they still be famous in five years' time? Why? / Why not?

2 Are you interested in famous people? Who are you a fan of? How do you find out about them?

3 With a partner, guess the answers to the questions below by choosing A, B or C.

A Emma Watson
B Cesc Fabregas
C Shakira

1 Who was born in 1987?
2 Who met President Obama in 2010?
3 Who has a French grandmother?
4 Who recorded an album at the age of 13?
5 Who went to a football match as a baby?

Grammar   Review of tenses

4 Choose the correct tense.

1 Shakira *has sold / sold* almost 60 million albums since her first one.
2 In 2010, Emma Watson *has become / became* Hollywood's highest paid female star.
3 I think Cesc Fabregas *won't play / doesn't play* again for Arsenal.
4 Shakira loved listening to 'merengue' dance music when she *was growing up / grew up* in Colombia.
5 Emma Watson *talks / is talking* to her co-star Daniel Radcliffe quite often.

G → page 148

5 Who are the most famous man and woman in your country today? Write sentences about them, saying:
  – when and where they were born
  – what has happened in their lives
  – how they became famous
  – what they are doing at the moment
  – what their lives will be like in five years' time.

6 Tick any tenses you have used in your sentences in exercise 5.

present simple   past continuous
present continuous   present perfect
past simple   future with *will*

Reading

7 Read the article about Emma Watson. Then answer the questions by choosing A, B or C.

EMMA WATSON

Emma Watson and Daniel Radcliffe at the opening of a *Harry Potter* film

Even as a child, Emma Watson wanted to be an actor. From the age of six, she was learning how to dance and sing after school, and was in many school plays. Her first paid acting job was as Hermione in the *Harry Potter* films. She didn't know then how big this project would be!

She often missed school because of *Harry Potter* but she and her co-stars had lessons each day at the places they were filming. She got excellent marks in her exams, which meant she could go to university anywhere. She chose the USA because she could study various subjects together, instead of just one in Britain.

Her student years have been fun and being famous hasn't given her many problems. She's had to speak to journalists since she was nine, so answering students' questions is OK – but she doesn't want her friends to see her as different, which most of them have understood.

Emma earned more than ten million pounds from her *Harry Potter* work and will never need to work for money again. However, she still enjoys acting, as well as working in fashion, which she feels she understands because of her art studies at school.

Daniel Radcliffe (Harry) is special to Emma. During the filming of *Harry Potter* he always understood his job as an actor, but what mattered to her was that he kept everyone else interested in the whole project. Daniel says they are 'very much like brother and sister'.

1 When she was 6, Emma
 A was already able to dance well.
 B took extra lessons outside school.
 C started singing in a school band.

2 Before she played Hermione in *Harry Potter*, Emma
 A earned money from other acting.
 B knew exactly how much work it was.
 C was only in school plays.

3 While she was filming *Harry Potter*, Emma
 A was usually able to get to her school.
 B spent part of her day in a special class.
 C had to study everything by herself.

4 Why did Emma choose to study in the USA?
 A She preferred the courses in American universities.
 B Her marks weren't good enough to study in Britain.
 C The one subject she wanted to study was only available there.

5 During her time at university, Emma
 A has spent a lot of time with journalists.
 B has hated being such a well-known actor.
 C has been able to enjoy a normal life.

6 Why is Emma happy to work in fashion?
 A She has become a bit bored with acting.
 B She needs to earn more money as an adult.
 C She knows something about it after studying art.

7 The article says that Daniel Radcliffe is important to Emma
 A because of what he has done for the *Harry Potter* project.
 B because she thinks of him more as a brother than a friend.
 C because he helped her to understand how to be a better actor.

8 Find examples in the article of five of the tenses listed in exercise 6. Which one isn't included?

UNIT 20 PEOPLE

20.2 Lucky people

1. Do you believe that some people have better luck than others? Why? / Why not?
2. Sports stars often do strange things, like asking for the same tennis ball, putting drinks bottles down in a certain way, or wearing the same shirt. Why do they do this? Can you think of other examples?
3. Answer the questions in this chart.

4. You have had some good luck and have won a competition. Your prize is to visit the city of your choice with one other person. Where will you go? Why? Who will you take?

Listening

5. 🔊 2 30 You will hear a girl called Ruth phoning a radio station about a prize she has won. Listen and complete questions 1–5.

Pronunciation

6. 🔊 2 31 Listen again to how Ruth asks these questions. Underline the word she stresses most in each one.
   1. What have I won?
   2. When do we have to use them by?
   3. Will you send me the tickets?
   4. Where are you?
   5. When shall I come?
   6. What time?

Speaking

7. Now it's your turn to ask questions.
   Student A should turn to page 133.
   Student B should turn to page 135.

Vocabulary

8 Read the descriptions of some adjectives about people. What is the word for each one? What is the adjective in the yellow box? Explain what it means.

1 Your best friend is this, because they are more important to you than other people. s _ _ _ _ _ _
2 Those who help other people are said to be this. k _ _ _
3 This word describes someone who is not married. s _ _ _ _ _
4 Anyone who gets excellent marks at school is this. c _ _ _ _ _
5 If you are laughing, this is how you feel. h _ _ _ _

Reading

9 Read the sentences about a teenage millionaire. Choose the best word (A, B or C) for each space.

1 Jason Richards has always .... to play computer games.
 A enjoyed
 B loved
 C invited

2 When he was 15, he had a good .... for a new game.
 A example
 B study
 C idea

3 Jason went to several computer .... to talk about his game.
 A stations
 B companies
 C houses

4 Nobody was .... in selling Jason's game.
 A interested
 B ready
 C pleased

5 Jason .... to sell his game himself on the internet.
 A thought
 B agreed
 C decided

6 In less than a year, Jason .... over £1,000,000 in sales.
 A earned
 B paid
 C spent

Spelling spot

ck or k?

- If the vowel before the /k/ sound is short, the spelling is 'ck': *back luck*
- With a short double vowel before the /k/ sound, there is no 'c': *look*
- If the vowel sound is long, there is no 'c': *break like*
- If a vowel is followed by a consonant, there is no 'c': *milk bank*

10 Sort the letters in these words and use them in the sentences below.

o o b   k j   c i k
g i   a c   n e
 k n   t e   h c

 k o   l   c t i
  l   u y   s k
 c c   k c   t e

1 There's something good on TV at nine o'............... .
2 Can I borrow your .... to wear to the theatre?
3 Let's phone the .... office now and get some .... for the festival.
4 How .... are you! You've won first prize again!
5 This .... and rice dish is wonderful. Is there any more?

Activity

Millionaire quiz

Answer your teacher's questions and win money for your team!

Units 17–20 Revision

Speaking

1 Ask and answer these questions with a partner.

1 Why do people go on diets?
2 What will you do if you pass *Cambridge English Key*?
3 Where is the city of Salamanca?
4 Which film actors or directors have won an Oscar?
5 Who do you think you will see next weekend?
6 How much fruit do you eat in a week?
7 When is your birthday?
8 What time will today's lesson finish?

Grammar

2 Match a phrase from A with a phrase from B and make conditional sentences.

EXAMPLE: *If I buy a new phone, I'll be able to send photos.*

A	B
1 buy a new phone	invite all my friends
2 get a Saturday job	visit some new websites
3 become famous	go out with my friends
4 eat more healthily	be able to send photos
5 have a party	earn some money
6 do all my homework	get a cup of coffee
7 go on the internet	feel better
8 take a break soon	build a house with a pool

3 Correct any wrong prepositions in this text about the island of Martinique.

Martinique is the largest island on the area of the eastern Caribbean. Over 300,000 people live at the island – many on the capital city, Fort-de-France. People speak French and it is taught on schools.

The mountains on Martinique are old volcanoes. The highest one is Mount Pelée, which is 1,397 metres high. At 1902, Mount Pelée erupted and about 30,000 people were killed.

The weather at Martinique is warm and quite wet – perfect for the farmers to grow bananas in their land. Bananas from Martinique are sent all over the world, so look at the bananas on your fruit bowl. If they are from Martinique, they will have a blue sticker in them.

Vocabulary

4 Decide which word is the odd one out.

1 laptop   internet   robot   website
2 ear   mouth   eye   back
3 email   letter   postcard envelope
4 German   Japanese   Italian   Spanish
5 prize   exam   test   competition
6 lucky   happy   special   ready

5 Read the sentences about recording a TV programme. Choose the best word (A, B or C) for each space.

1 I wanted to .... a football match on the TV.
   A take   B look   C watch

2 My sister was .... with me because there was a programme about lions on at the same time.
   A upset   B sorry   C difficult

3 She .... me to record the programme for her.
   A invited   B asked   C decided

4 By mistake, I chose the .... TV channel.
   A bad   B wrong   C open

5 My sister was mad when she .... there was a history programme instead of the one about lions.
   A found   B turned   C kept

Writing

6 Read questions A and B and decide which sentences (1–6 below) go with each question. Then put each set of sentences in order, adding a few more words to make a 35-word email that answers each question.

A

You saw someone famous when you were in your capital city last week.
Write an email to your friend, saying:
- which famous person you saw
- where you were at the time
- how you felt.

B

You would like to invite your friend to a party.
Write an email to your friend, saying:
- when you are going to have the party
- who else you have invited
- what you would like your friend to bring.

1 Heidi and Lorna can come as well.
2 It was amazing and I couldn't believe it!
3 Could I borrow some of your party albums?
4 It'll be on Saturday 15th November, starting at 8.30 p.m.
5 Tom Cruise walked by just in front of me.
6 I was looking at a painting in an art gallery.

Extra material

1.2 Activity

Questionnaire

Name	
Age	
Address	
Favourite music	
Favourite place(s)	
What makes you laugh?	

3.1 Activity

Question	Student 1	Student 2	Student 3 ....
What time do you get up?	At	At	At
What do you have for breakfast?			
What time do you have lunch?	At	At	At
What do you prefer for lunch?			
What time do you have dinner?	At	At	At
What do you like best for dinner?			

6.2 Activity

Group A

How often do you watch TV?

every night   only at weekends   not often

What is your favourite free-time activity at home?

playing music   reading books
playing chess   seeing friends
playing computer games   something else

What is your least favourite free-time activity at home?

....

Add some more questions here:

....
....
....
....

Group B

What is your favourite free-time physical activity?

football   swimming
tennis   skateboarding
running   something else

....

How often do you do a physical activity?

every day   three times a week
once a week   less than once a week

What is your least favourite free-time physical activity?

....

Add some more questions here:

....
....
....

Exam folder 5

Candidate B questions

Holiday Centre

★ where?

★ what / do?

★ price / adult?

★ open / all year?

★ place / eat?

EXTRA MATERIAL 131

9.2 Activity

ARE YOU A WORLD TRAVELLER?

1 **How often do you go on holiday?**
   A hardly ever
   B once a year
   C twice a year or more

2 **How many countries have you visited?**
   A two
   B none
   C six or more

3 **You win the lottery – where will you go?**
   A to Disney World for a month
   B to an expensive hotel in my country
   C on a trip round the world

4 **What type of holiday do you like?**
   A staying at home doing nothing
   B activity holidays such as sailing
   C lying on a sandy beach and dancing at night

5 **Your hotel room isn't very nice. Do you**
   A complain to the manager?
   B not worry about it?
   C not notice?

6 **What do you buy on holiday?**
   A presents for all your friends
   B one or two souvenirs
   C some sweets for yourself

7 **Do you send postcards?**
   A no – never
   B yes – to everyone I know
   C yes – to a few friends

8 **Who do you like to go on holiday with?**
   A no one – I prefer to be alone
   B my best friend
   C my family

Now turn to page 134 to find your score.

EXTRA MATERIAL

11.1 Exercise 9

College Sports Day

College Sports Field
Saturday 12 June (10.00–3.30)

Football, volleyball and running for everyone.

Win one of 50 T-shirts!

Don't forget your shorts and trainers!

Exam folder 5

Candidate A questions

Cinema
- what / see?
- film / start?
- eat?
- what / address?
- student ticket / £?

16.2 Exercise 4

Student A questions

DAY TRIP FOR STUDENTS
- where?
- when?
- cost?
- transport?
- things to do?

20.2 Exercise 7

Student A questions

Ask Student B about his/her favourite holiday place.

What … favourite holiday place?
Where …?
How … get there?
What … like best about it?

9.2 Activity

Key

1	A 1	B 2	C 3
2	A 2	B 1	C 3
3	A 2	B 1	C 3
4	A 1	B 2	C 3
5	A 3	B 2	C 1
6	A 3	B 2	C 1
7	A 1	B 3	C 2
8	A 3	B 2	C 1

World Traveller 21–24 points
You really like holidays and enjoy everything about them: buying presents, seeing friends and having fun. But remember, you can have fun at home too!

Happy Tourist 12–20 points
You like to go to new places. You enjoy quiet holidays with a few friends and you prefer not to spend too much money.

Stay-at-Home 8–11 points
You quite like going away, but you prefer to be with people you know. You are also happy at home. You believe holidays should be relaxing.

16.2 Exercise 4

Student B answers

HAVE FUN ON OUR SCHOOL TRIP TO BRIGHTON

Only £12.50 for students at this school!

Price includes lunch and return coach journey

Free time for shopping or visiting the beach

Saturday 7 April (book by Wednesday 4 April)

16.2 Exercise 5

Student B's questions

Hiking trip
- date?
- price?
- how far?
- what clothes?
- things to take?

EXTRA MATERIAL

18.2 Exercise 1

Question	Name	Name	Name ....
1 How many hours a night do you sleep?			
2 How many hours did you sleep last night?			
3 Do you sleep on your back, your side or your front?			
4 Do you remember your dreams?			
5 Have you ever had a bad dream?			
6 What do you do if you wake up in the night?			
7 What do you do if you have problems getting to sleep?			

16.2 Exercise 5

Student A's answers

TAKE SOME EXERCISE ON OUR FULL-DAY HIKING TRIP!
20-kilometre path in the beautiful Hassett Hills

Bring a water bottle and picnic food
Dress for rain and wind!

Saturday April 14, bus leaves 7.15 (back 21.00)
£13.75 including transport

20.2 Exercise 7

Student B questions

Ask Student A about his/her luckiest moment.

What … was your luckiest moment?
When … happen?
Why … happen?
How … feel?
What … do afterwards?

19.2 Exercise 5

	Monday	Tuesday	Wednesday	Thursday	Friday
9.00	German Grammar		Russian Reading		Russian Grammar
10.00		German Writing			Russian Writing
11.00			Russian Conversation		
12.00	Russian Listening			German Reading	
1.00			LUNCH		
2.00				German Listening	
3.00	German Conversation				

EXTRA MATERIAL

Grammar folder

Unit 1

Yes/No questions in the present

- With **have got**, *have* comes first and *got* comes after the subject.
  Have you **got** any money with you?
- With **be**, the verb comes first.
  Is Giulio one of your friends?
- With **can**, this verb comes first and the main verb comes after the subject.
  Can I borrow your music magazine?
- With **other verbs**, we start the question with *Do* or *Does* and the main verb comes after the subject.
  Do you **want** a cup of coffee?
  Does Sandro **help** you with your homework?

1A Change the word order to make Yes/No questions.

1. got / my phone / you / have
   Have you got my phone?
2. tomorrow / your sister / come / can
3. Carmen and Maria / are / Brazil / from
4. like / dogs / you / do
5. it / time / to go / is
6. Arturo / catch / does / the same bus

Wh- questions in the present

- With **be**, **have got** and **can**, the verb comes after the question word.
  What's the time?
  Who **have** you **got** in your maths class?
  How **can** I get to your house?
- With **other verbs**, *do* or *does* comes after the question word. The subject comes next and the main verb comes after the subject.
  Why **do** you **want** my phone number?
  When **does** Jana **get** home?

1B Make Wh- questions. Add the subject *you* if you need it.

1. When / meet me / can
   When can you meet me?
2. How / get to school / do
3. Where / your house / is
4. What / in your bag / have got
5. Why / angry / are
6. Who / know / Ingrid / does

Suggestions

- We use **Why don't/doesn't ...** to make suggestions.
  Why don't we meet at school?
  Why doesn't Ruth come with us?
- We also use **How about ...** to make suggestions. (Use the *-ing* verb after *How about*.)
  How about seeing a film tonight?

Unit 2

Some/any

- We use **some** with uncountable nouns in affirmative sentences.
  *I've got **some** chocolate.*

- We use **some** with countable nouns in affirmative sentences.
  *That shop has got **some** new computer games.*

- We use **some** for a request.
  *Can I look at **some** trainers?*

- We always use **any** in negative sentences.
  *We don't sell **any** magazines here.*

- We usually use **any** in questions.
  *Have you got **any** city maps?*

2 Complete the sentences with *some* or *any*.

1. I'd like ..*some*.. tennis balls, please.
2. There aren't .... cheap DVDs here.
3. Have you got .... shops near your flat?
4. Can I buy .... apples?
5. I want .... lemon shampoo.
6. Is there .... juice left?
7. We've got .... cameras in the sale.
8. Do you get .... emails about online shopping?

Unit 3

Present simple

We use the present simple to talk about:

- what we do every day
  *I **have breakfast** at 7.30 a.m.*

- facts
  *Bookshops often **sell** birthday cards.
  Cats **eat** fish.*

affirmative
I/You/We/They **drink** coffee. He/She/It **drinks** water.

question
What **do** I/you/we/they eat? What **does** he/she/it drink?

negative
I/You/We/They **don't eat (do not eat)** potatoes. He/She/It **doesn't drink (does not drink)** water.

3A Complete the sentences using the verb in brackets.

1. I ..*prefer*.. (prefer) coffee to tea.
2. .... Pete really .... (hate) carrots?
3. Both Katie and Jack .... (love) chocolate.
4. My brother .... (not eat) fish.
5. Rafael .... (go) to restaurants three times a week.
6. .... you usually .... (go) to a party at New Year?
7. Supermarkets .... (not sell) computers.

Telling the time

Asking the time	Saying what the time is
What time is it? What's the time? Could you tell me the time, please?	It's ... 7.05 seven (oh) five *or* five past seven 7.10 seven ten *or* ten past seven 7.15 seven fifteen *or* (a) quarter past seven 7.25 seven twenty-five *or* twenty-five past seven 7.30 seven thirty *or* half past seven 7.35 seven thirty-five *or* twenty-five to eight 7.45 seven forty-five *or* (a) quarter to eight 7.50 seven fifty *or* ten to eight 8.00 eight o'clock

For other times, for example 7.03, 7.17, 7.43, we say <u>minutes</u> to/past seven/eight:
three minutes past seven
twenty-seven minutes to eight

3B Match the times with the clocks.

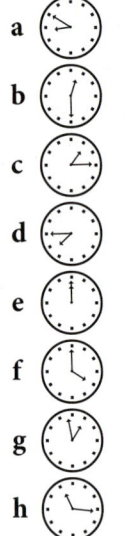

1 one fifteen   *c*
2 two minutes to one
3 quarter to eight
4 ten to nine
5 midday
6 sixteen minutes past eleven
7 half past twelve
8 four o'clock

Unit 4

Past simple

We use the past simple to talk about:
- things that happened in the past
  *Men **travelled** from all over the world.*
- past states
  *He **liked** gold.*

The verb *be*

affirmative
I/He/She/It **was** right. You/We/They **were** right.

question
Was I/he/she/it right? **Were** you/we/they right? Yes, I/he/she/it **was**. Yes, you/we/they **were**. No, I/he/she/it **wasn't (was not)**. No, you/we/they **weren't (were not)**.

negative
I/He/She/It **wasn't (was not)** right. You/We/They **weren't (were not)** right.

Regular verbs, e.g. *arrive*

affirmative
I/You/He/She/It/We/They **arrived** home.

question
Did I/you/he/she/it/we/they **arrive** home? Yes, I/you/he/she/it/we/they **did**. No, I/you/he/she/it/we/they **didn't (did not)**.

Irregular verbs, e.g. *see*

Many verbs are irregular in the past tense, for example *see – saw*. See the list on page 159.

affirmative
I/You/He/She/It/We/They **saw** Skookum Jim.

question
Did I/you/he/she/it/we/they **see** Skookum Jim? Yes, I/you/he/she/it/we/they **did**. No, I/you/he/she/it/we/they **didn't (did not)**.

negative
I/You/He/She/It/We/They **didn't see** Skookum Jim.

4 Complete the sentences using the verb in brackets in the past simple.

1. How long *did you stay* (you stay) in London?
2. .... (you enjoy) the boat trip?
3. The coach .... (not arrive) back at school on time.
4. My mother .... (make) me some sandwiches for the trip.
5. We .... (travel) to Rome by plane.
6. What .... (Lyn see) in India?
7. When .... (Pete go) to Peru?
8. He .... (not speak) Spanish on his holiday.
9. How much .... (she spend) on holiday?
10. Where .... (she buy) that present?

Unit 5

Conjunctions

and but or because

We use conjunctions to join two clauses or sentences to make one longer sentence.

Sentence A   *Polar bears weigh from 350 to 650 kg.*   **AND**
Sentence B   *Polar bears are two and a half to three metres long.*

Polar bears weigh from 350 to 650 kg and are two and a half to three metres long.

- We use **and** when we want to *add* one fact or idea to another.
  *I saw a polar bear **and** there were two cubs with her.*
- We use **but** when there is a *contrast* between the two facts or ideas.
  *I saw a polar bear **but** he was asleep.*
- We use **or** when there is a *choice* or an alternative fact or idea.
  *You can go to the zoo **or** stay at home.*
- We use **because** to say *why* things happen.
  *I gave the cat some fish **because** it was hungry.*
  ***Because** the cat was hungry, I gave it some fish.*

5 Complete these sentences using *and, but, or* or *because*.

1. Dogs like going for long walks *and* also playing with balls.
2. My cat is getting old, ... she still climbs walls.
3. I took my dog to the park .... she needed a walk.
4. Elephants in India work in the early morning .... sleep in the afternoon.
5. .... I live in a flat, I can't have a pet.
6. Would you like a cat as a pet .... do you prefer dogs?

GRAMMAR FOLDER 139

Unit 6

Comparative and superlative adjectives

adjective	comparative	superlative
short words		
tall	taller	the tallest
big	bigger	the biggest
easy	easier	the easiest
long words		
expensive	more/less expensive	the most/least expensive
exceptions		
good	better	the best
bad	worse	the worst

*Theme parks in the USA are **bigger than** the ones in the UK.*
*My ticket was **more expensive** this year **than** last.*
*I think Disneyland is **the best** theme park.*

6 Complete these sentences with either the comparative or the superlative form of the adjective in brackets.

1. The park was ......*busier*...... (busy) on Saturday than on Sunday.
2. Children's tickets are usually .... (expensive) than adults' tickets.
3. The ride I went on was .... (tall) in the park.
4. My uncle is .... (rich) than I am, so he paid for my trip to Disneyland Paris.
5. It was .... (sunny) on Tuesday than it was on Monday.
6. .... (popular) ride was in Japan.
7. The ride was .... (fast) in the park.
8. The theme park was .... (expensive) than the one I usually go to.
9. Some theme parks are .... (good) than others.
10. Our hotel was .... (bad) in the area.

Unit 7

Simple and continuous tenses

- We use the **present continuous** to talk about **something temporary**, that is true now but not in general. Compare these sentences:
  I'm wearing a skirt today because I've got an interview.
  I usually wear jeans.

- We can use the **past continuous** to talk about a **temporary situation in the past**. Compare this with the **past simple**, which we use for a **completed action**:
  Most people were wearing Roma shirts at last week's match.
  Roma won last week's match 2–0.

- We also use the **past continuous** to talk about **something which continued before or after** another action.
  I was shopping for shoes when my mobile phone rang.

7 Put the verbs in brackets in the correct past tense.

1. Helena ......*was looking at*...... (look at) jackets when I ......*met*...... (meet) her.
2. I .... (try on) some new earrings when I .... (lose) one.
3. John .... (wait) to pay when he .... (remember) his wallet was at home.
4. Martina .... (choose) her meal when the fire alarm .... (start).
5. Maria .... (study) in the garden when it .... (begin) to rain.
6. When my friend .... (phone), I .... (have) a shower, so she .... (leave) me a message.

GRAMMAR FOLDER

Unit 8

Modal verbs 1

must and *have to*

- In the present, we use **must** and **have to** to talk about obligation.
  You **must** finish your homework before you go out.
  James **has to** work at the hotel every night this week.

- In the past, we cannot use **must**. Instead, we use **had to**.
  I **had to** queue for twenty minutes at the cinema.

may and *might*

- We use **may** and **might** to talk about possibility.
  I **may** come with you tonight.
  There **might** be some tickets left for the concert.

can and *could*

- In the present, we use **can** to talk about ability.
  I **can** ride a bike. (= I know how to ride a bike.)
  I **can't** drive. (= I don't know how to drive.)

- In the past tense, we use **could** and **couldn't**.
  Sam **could** play the guitar before he was 12.
  He **couldn't** read music when he was at school.

8 Complete the sentences using each modal verb once only.

| can   can't   ~~couldn't~~   has to   had to |
| may   might   must |

1 Giacomo didn't know how to find the cinema.
  Giacomo _couldn't_ find the cinema.

2 Perhaps I'll borrow that DVD from Jo.
  I .... borrow that DVD from Jo.

3 Don't forget to wear a white shirt and black trousers for tonight's concert.
  You .... remember to wear a white shirt and black trousers for tonight's concert.

4 Sorry, I'm busy next Friday, so it's not possible to go out.
  I .... go out next Friday because I'm busy.

5 The front door of the club was shut.
  We .... use the back door of the club.

6 The singer can't do tonight's show because she's flying home early.
  The singer .... fly home early, so she can't do tonight's show.

7 Does the theatre website have more information, maybe?
  The theatre .... have more information on its website.

8 I know how to play the drums.
  I .... play the drums.

GRAMMAR FOLDER 141

Unit 9

The future with *going to*

- We use *to be going to* to talk about plans and arrangements which are definite.

affirmative		
I	am	
He/She/It	is	going to swim every day.
You/We/They	are	

question		
Am	I	
Is	he/she/it	going to walk up the hill?
Are	you/we/they	

negative		
I	'm not	
He/she/it	isn't	going to sleep in a tent.
We/you/they	aren't	

question		
Aren't I/we/you/they		
Isn't he/she		going to book a room?
Note: Am I not becomes Aren't I.		

I'**m going to** stay in Tokyo when I'm in Japan.
He **isn't going to** spend a lot of money on an expensive hotel.
Sam's **going to** take one small suitcase with him when he goes on holiday next week.

The future with *will*

- We use *will* to give information about the future or guess what will happen in the future.

affirmative and negative
I/you/he/she/it/we/they will / will not (won't) travel.

question and negative
Will/won't I/you/he/she/it/we/they travel?

One day people **will** live on the Moon.

- We often use *will* with sentences beginning *I think …* and with adverbs like *certainly* (100%), *definitely* (100%), *probably* (about 70%) and *possibly* (about 40%).
I think I will / I'll get a holiday job next year.
I will / I'll probably work in a hotel.
I don't think I'll earn a lot of money.
I probably won't spend a lot of money.

9 Use *be going to* or *will* in these sentences.

1. I ……*am going to*…… go to Sicily for my holidays next month – I already have my ticket.
2. Congratulations! I hear you and Theresa ……………………………… get married.
3. What ……………………………… you study when you go to university?
4. I ……………………………… have a party on Saturday – do you want to come?
5. The Lunar Hotel ……………………………… probably be the first hotel in space.
6. Claire thinks she ……………………………… definitely go to Australia next year.
7. Maria ……………………………… fly to South Africa next week and she's very excited.
8. I don't think people ……………………………… enjoy living on the moon very much.
9. I think flying ……………………………… become much cheaper in the future.
10. Maria ……………………………… buy a new camera for her holiday.

Unit 10

The passive

present simple passive	am/is/are (not)	+ past participle painted
past simple passive	was/were (not)	seen built made

The sentence *I painted my bedroom black* is active.
The sentence *My bedroom was painted black* is passive.

- We often use **by** with the passive to tell us who did the action.
  *My bedroom was painted **by** my father.*
- The past participle of regular verbs ends in *-ed*, like the past tense.
- See page 159 for a list of past participles of irregular verbs.

10 Make sentences in the passive using A, B and C.

EXAMPLE: *The song 'Imagine' was sung by John Lennon.*

	A	B	C
1	The song 'Imagine'	stop	by J. K. Rowling.
2	Portuguese	give	in sweet shops.
3	The Pyramids	win	to swim by my father.
4	The *Harry Potter* books	sing	by Spain in 2010.
5	Presents	sell	in Brazil.
6	Spaghetti	teach	by John Lennon.
7	I	build	on birthdays.
8	Chocolate	eat	by the Egyptians.
9	The World Cup	speak	all over the world.
10	The car	write	by the police.

Unit 11

Verbs in the *-ing* form

- The *-ing* form is added to the infinitive of the verb:
  play + -ing = playing   *I enjoy **playing** tennis.*
- Different groups of verbs are followed by a verb in the *-ing* form:
  - verbs of liking and disliking:
    enjoy, like*, love*, hate, don't mind
    *Sam hates **losing** tennis matches.*
  - verbs of doing:
    keep, spend time
    *He kept **asking** questions.*
    *We spent the day **fishing**.*
  - verbs of starting and stopping:
    begin*, start*, finish, stop
    *We finished **playing** just before lunchtime.*
    *They stopped **talking** immediately.*

* these verbs can also take an infinitive with no change of meaning:
  *I like **to listen** to the football scores at 5 o'clock.*
  *The team starts **to train** harder two days before a match.*

11 Complete the sentences with the *-ing* form of the verb in brackets.

1. I don't mind *coming* (come) with you to basketball training.
2. I spent yesterday afternoon .... (swim) – what did you do?
3. Harry likes .... (choose) the team himself.
4. Do you enjoy .... (use) the gym equipment?
5. Kate hates .... (sit) and .... (watch) – she prefers to play in every match.
6. I hope Jenny doesn't mind .... (get) wet – it's going to rain!
7. How about .... (run) in the park before dinner?
8. Dan enjoys .... (ride) his horse every morning.

GRAMMAR FOLDER

Unit 12

Pronouns

- There are different forms of personal pronouns:

subject pronouns	object pronouns	reflexive pronouns
I	me	myself
you	you	yourself
he, she, it	him, her, it	himself, herself, itself
we	us	ourselves
you	you	yourselves
they	them	themselves

- These are also pronouns:

things	people
something	somebody / someone
anything	anybody / anyone
everything	everybody / everyone
nothing	nobody / no one

- Remember that you must use a positive verb with *nothing*, *nobody* and *no one*.
  I've got nothing to read on the train.
  (= **I haven't got anything** to read on the train.)

12 Complete the second sentences using suitable pronouns from those above.

1 Jenny came to the party alone.
  Jenny didn't come with ……*anyone*…… .
2 David knows what happened.
  I've told David ………………… .
3 There's a phone message for you.
  ………………… from work called you.
4 I'm sure I can help.
  There must be ………………… I can do.
5 All my family came to the party.
  ………………… in my family was at the party.
6 The bus was empty.
  There was ………………… on the bus.

Unit 13

Adverbs of degree: *enough* and *too*

adjective + *enough*
I don't want to go swimming. It isn't **hot enough**.
***too* + adjective**
Can you close the window? It's **too cold** in here.

- We can also use *to* + infinitive after *too* and *enough* with adjectives or adverbs.
  It's hot enough **to fry** an egg.
  It's too far **to walk**.

13 Complete the sentences with *too* or *enough* and the adjective in brackets.

1 It's ……*too dangerous*…… (dangerous) to go outside if there's a tornado.
2 It's ………………… (dry) here to grow tomatoes.
3 It's ………………… (wet) to go for a walk.
4 The sun isn't ………………… (hot) to heat the water in the pool.
5 It isn't ………………… (cold) to wear a coat.
6 The wind was ………………… (strong) to go sailing.

Unit 14

Position of adjectives

- Sometimes we use two or more adjectives together. We put the 'opinion' adjective(s) first, and the 'fact' adjective(s) after.
  The story is about a nice young man.
- If there is more than one fact adjective, there are rules about the order they go in.

1 What's it like? opinion	2 How big? size	3 How old? age	4 What colour?	5 Where's it from? nationality	6 What kind?	NOUN
great		new			electric	guitar
	tall			American		boy
	large		white			house

14 Put the adjectives in brackets in the correct place.

1 a old building (lovely)
  a lovely old building
2 a wooden reading desk (large)
3 a popular American magazine (music)
4 an interesting story (adventure)
5 a friendly detective (young)
6 my French comic book (favourite)

Unit 15

Present perfect

- The present perfect is formed with:
  have ('ve) / has ('s) + past participle
  I **have worked** as a waiter.
  I've seen an interesting job advert.
  The manager **has sent** me an application form.
- Be careful with the past participle forms of irregular verbs! See the table on page 159.
- We use the present perfect
  – for something that started in the past but is still true:
    I've broken my arm. (= it's still broken)
  – for something that happened recently (but we don't know when):
    Alan's left for work.
- The words *for* and *since* show how long something has been true:
  I've worked here **for** four months.
  I've worked here **since** August.

- The word *just* shows that something happened only a short time ago:
  The bus has **just** gone.

15 Rewrite these sentences using the present perfect and *just*.

1 Tyler began working as a chef last week.
  Tyler has just begun working as a chef.
2 Joan took the customer's order five minutes ago.
3 Giorgio recently became a doctor.
4 Someone left a message for you a couple of minutes ago.
5 I saw our dentist crossing the street a few seconds ago.
6 I spoke to the engineer on the phone a few minutes ago.

Unit 16

Modal verbs 2

should

- We can use **should** (and **shouldn't**) to give advice.
  You **should** walk to school – it's good exercise.
  You **shouldn't** come by car – it's better to walk.

must and have to

- We use **must** and **have to** to talk about obligation.
  You **must** buy a ticket before you get on the bus.
  We **had to** take a taxi because we missed the bus.

- We use **mustn't** to talk about things that aren't allowed.
  You **mustn't** get on the bus without a ticket.

need to

- We use **need to** to talk about something necessary.
  You **need to** check the train times on Saturdays.

don't have to and needn't

- We use **don't have to** and **needn't** when something is not necessary (when there is no obligation).
  You **don't have to** show your ticket to the driver.
  You **needn't** wait for me on the platform. I'll see you on the train.

16 Find the pairs of sentences that have the same meaning.

1 You don't have to book a seat on the flight. *6*
2 You mustn't make any phone calls during the flight.
3 You should take something to read on the flight.
4 You need to arrive early for the flight.
5 You cannot use your mobile during the flight.
6 You needn't book a place on the flight. *1*
7 You shouldn't arrive just before the flight leaves.
8 Why not bring a book for the flight?

Unit 17

Infinitive of purpose

- We often use the infinitive (**to** + **verb**) to say *why* we do things.
  Liz needed a new bed.
  She went to a large department store.
  Liz went to a large department store **to buy** a new bed.

17 Make one sentence using a phrase from A and a phrase from B.

EXAMPLE: *I went to the bus stop to catch a bus to town.*

A	B
1 I went to the bus stop	to pass the exam.
2 I turned on the radio	to buy a computer game.
3 I went to the museum	to take to the party.
4 I borrowed some money	to see an exhibition.
5 I worked hard	to listen to the news.
6 I bought a cake	to catch a bus to town.

146 GRAMMAR FOLDER

Unit 18

First conditional

- The first conditional is formed with:
  If + present tense + *will* + infinitive
- We use this structure to express a possible condition.
  ***If** he **goes** swimming every day, he**'ll get fit**.*
  (comma after the 'if' clause)
  We can also say:
  *He**'ll get fit** if he **goes** swimming every day.*
  (no comma)

18 Complete these sentences.

1 If you (sleep) __sleep__ with the window open, you (sleep much better) __you'll sleep much better__ .

2 If you (eat) .... an apple a day, you (not get ill) ....

3 If you (not eat) .... too many sweets, you (not get fat) ....

4 You (lose) .... weight if you (stop eating snacks) ....

5 Your teeth (stay) .... healthy if you (visit the dentist) .... once a year.

6 You (have) .... bad dreams if you (eat cheese in the evening) ....

Unit 19

Prepositions of place

- We use **at** to talk about a specific place:
  *We're meeting **at** the stadium.*
  *Who's that **at** the bus stop?*
- We also use **at** to talk about places where you study or work:
  *Jane's studying Greek **at** university.*
- We use **on** to talk about where something is:
  *My bag is **on** the table.*
  *There's another bottle of lemonade **on** the shelf.*
- We can use **in** or **on** with street names (but not for addresses):
  *The bookshop's **in** Bridge Street.*
  *I live **on** Madison Avenue.*
  *I live **at** 495 Madison Avenue.*
- We use **in** to talk about where something is:
  *There's a present for you **in** this box.*
  *Carrie's **in** the garden if you want to speak to her.*
- We use **in** with cities and countries:
  *I studied French **in** Paris.*
  *Uppsala is **in** Sweden.*

19A Complete the sentences with *at*, *in* or *on*.

1 I left my coat __on__ the chair. Could you get it?
2 Where's Punta Arenas? – It's .... Chile.
3 I'm meeting Sam .... the college gates.
4 Robert is living .... London.
5 How long will you be .... work?
   – I won't be free before six.
6 There's a new jazz club .... Hilton Road.
7 We're living .... 16 Pinewood Road until April.
8 Is that your pen .... the floor?
9 Nick is studying Biology .... Leeds University.
10 How much is the red guitar .... the window?

Prepositions of time

- We use **at** with exact times, periods of time, meals and festivals:
  *Come round **at** five o'clock.*
  *We'll be free **at** the weekend.*
  *Kelly sat with John **at** breakfast.*
  *I'm doing a French course **at** Easter.*

- We use **in** with centuries, years, months, seasons and parts of the day:
  *Cornish was spoken **in** the 18th century.*
  *The book first came out **in** 2003.*
  *I went to Milan **in** January.*
  *It gets very busy here **in** summer.*
  *Shall we meet **in** the morning?*

- We use **on** with days of the week, dates and special days:
  *I have Spanish classes **on** Tuesday and Thursday.*
  *The concert will be **on** 27th June.*
  *I always have a party **on** my birthday.*

19B Complete the sentences with *at*, *in* or *on*.

1 Will I see you __in__ March?
2 My birthday's _____ September 30th.
3 Dani's going to visit us _____ Christmas.
4 What do you like to do _____ the evening?
5 I can't go to the theatre _____ Saturday.
6 This house was built _____ 1872.
7 Your appointment is _____ 3.15.
8 You can't swim here _____ winter.

Unit 20
Review of tenses

Present simple
I like Daniel Radcliffe.
Most people wear jeans.
→ See Unit 3

Present continuous
I'm reading an adventure story.
→ See Unit 7

Past simple
Leonardo da Vinci designed a helicopter.
→ See Unit 4

Past continuous
We were having a picnic when it started to rain.
→ See Unit 7

Present perfect
I've just had a text message from my brother.
→ See Unit 15

Future with *will*
We'll meet in London for your birthday.
→ See Unit 9

Future with *going to*
I'm going to have a bath and go to bed.
→ See Unit 9

20 Complete the sentences in the correct tense, using a verb from the box.

| ask | drive | eat | go out | make | sing |
| stop | win | | | | |

1 Before she was famous, Pink __sang__ in an all-girl band called *Choice*.
2 Adele _____ a new album – it'll go on sale next month.
3 Do you think Zac Efron _____ with Lily Collins at the moment?
4 Barack Obama and the President of Russia _____ a burger after their meeting.
5 The police _____ Justin Timberlake when he _____ too fast.
6 Meryl Streep _____ an Oscar as Best Actress in 2012 for the film *The Iron Lady*.
7 While she is on tour, Katy Perry _____ for white and purple flowers to welcome her in every dressing room.

Vocabulary folder

Here is a list of words and phrases from each unit of Objective Key. Try to learn their spelling and how you can use them. Some words are in more than one unit, to help you remember them.

Unit 1

Things you do with friends
borrow a DVD/money, etc. from someone
chat about football, make-up, etc.
forget/remember a birthday, etc.
get/send a text message
go on the PlayStation
go shopping
lend someone a DVD/magazine, etc.
tell someone a lie

Asking and answering
OK …
Right …
So …
And …
Well …
That's easy.
That's difficult.
That's right.

Adjectives
amazing
angry
boring
free
funny
great
happy
horrible
ill
lucky
pleased
popular
sad
sick
special
true
worried
wrong

Unit 2

Places to go shopping
bookshop
chemist
department store
market
sports shop
supermarket

Things to buy – uncountable nouns
bread
cheese
chocolate
fish
ice cream
leather
make-up
medicine
money
pasta
shampoo
soap

Things to buy – countable nouns
apple
ball
birthday card
book
box (boxes)
DVD
camera
carrot
dish (dishes)
ice cream
magazine
map
potato (potatoes)
sandwich
shoes
sweets
T-shirt
tennis racket
tomato (tomatoes)
toy
trainers

Short phrases
No problem
Of course
OK
You're welcome

Unit 3

Food
apple
banana
beans
biscuits
bread
burger
cake
carrot
cheese
chicken
chilli
chips
chocolate
curry
egg
fish
fruit
grape
ice cream
meat
mushroom
onion
orange
pasta
pizza
potato
rice
salad
sandwich
soup
steak
tomato
yogurt

Drink
coffee
juice
lemonade
milk
tea
water

Meals
breakfast
lunch
dinner
snack

Verbs
drink
eat

Verb + noun
have a drink
have (a) pizza
make a meal

Unit 4

Regular verbs
(Irregular verbs see p151)
arrive
carry
decide
email
help
like
listen
look

VOCABULARY FOLDER 149

open
pick up
play
return
show
stay
stop
study
travel
use
visit
want
work

Unit 5

Animals
bear
bird
cat
chicken
cow
dog
duck
elephant
fish
horse
lion
monkey

Verb + noun
do homework
do nothing
do the cooking
do the shopping
make an appointment
make a cake
make a phone call
spend money
spend time
take a photograph
take an exam
take the dog for a walk

Unit 6

Adjectives
angry
attractive
bad
beautiful
big
boring
bright
cheap
closed
comfortable
easy
expensive
fast
good
happy
high
horrible
large
long
modern
new
old
open
popular
short
small
tall
thin
tidy

Adverbs
badly
carefully
cheaply
early
fast
hard
late
later
long
near
quietly
soon
well

Things you do in your free time
go to the cinema
go cycling
go dancing
go shopping
go skateboarding
go swimming
have a party
listen to music
play chess
play computer games
play table tennis
read comics
see friends
watch TV

Unit 7

Clothes
baseball cap
belt
boots (a pair of boots)
button
coat
dress
hat
jacket
jeans
pocket
shirt
shoes (a pair of shoes)
shorts (a pair of shorts)
size
skirt
socks
suit
sweater
T-shirt
trainers (a pair of trainers)
trousers (a pair of trousers)

Jewellery
earring (a pair of earrings)
necklace
ring

Adjectives
cheap
clean
cotton
dirty
expensive
gold
heavy
large
leather
light
long
new
old
silver
short
small
unfashionable
wool

Unit 8

Talking about films
actor
film
movie
scene
sound effects
story

Adjectives
amazing
awesome
excellent
exciting
famous
well-known

Music
album
band
bass
concert
drums
festival
guitar
lights
piano
singer
speakers

Short phrases
☹
Never mind.
That's bad.
That's a shame.
What a pity.

☺
Cool!
Fantastic!
Thanks a lot.
That's great!

Unit 9

Kinds of holiday
a beach/camping/
  cycling/sightseeing/
  walking holiday

Places
campsite
holiday home
holiday centre
hotel

Verbs
book a hotel, holiday
catch a plane, bus,
  train
go/travel by plane,
  by car, by boat
go sightseeing

Nouns
guidebook
journey
luggage
map
passport
suitcase
ticket
tour

Unit 10

The home
bathroom
bedroom
dining room
garage
hall
kitchen
living room

Things in a room
bed
bookshelf
carpet
chair
computer
curtains
desk
DVD player
floor
lamp
light
mirror
pillow
poster
sofa
TV
wardrobe

Materials
cotton
glass
gold
leather
metal
paper
plastic
silver
wood
wool

Adjectives
big
double
expensive
hard
high
little
long
low
narrow
new
quiet
short
single
soft
wide

Colours
black
blue
brown
green
grey
orange
pink
purple
red
white
yellow

Unit 11

Sports
baseball
basketball
football
horse-riding
sailing
skiing
snowboarding
surfing
swimming
volleyball

More sports words
ball
basket
bat
board
boots
competition
court
exercise
glove(s)
goal
match
net
racket
stadium
team

Unit 12

Family
aunt
brother
cousin
dad
daughter
father
grandchild
granddaughter
grandfather
  (granddad)
grandmother
  (grandma)
grandson
mother
mum
parent
sister
son
uncle

Unit 13

Weather
cloud(y)
cold
dry
fog(gy)
hot
ice/icy
rain(y)/raining
snow(y)
storm(y)
sun(ny)
tornado
warm
wet
wind(y)

Unit 14

Kinds of reading material
adventure story
book
comic
detective story
funny story
love story
picture book
science fiction book

Saying what you think
I think it's awesome,
  brilliant, cool, great.
It's horrible, terrible,
  boring, crazy, strange.
It isn't very exciting,
  interesting.
It's OK / all right.
It isn't boring.

VOCABULARY FOLDER

Subjects
art
geography
history
languages
maths
music
science
sport

Unit 15

Jobs
actor
chef
cleaner
dentist
doctor
engineer
farmer
footballer
journalist
nurse
photographer
police officer
receptionist
secretary
shop assistant
teacher
tennis player
tour guide
waiter

People at work
boss
colleague
manager
staff

Unit 16

Transport – nouns
airport
bicycle (bike)
boat
bus
car
coach
helicopter
horse
plane
ship
taxi
train

Transport – verbs
board
catch
drive
fly
get (on/off)
park
ride
sail
take off

Free-time activities – verb + noun
climb a hill
fly a kite
have a picnic
kick a football
throw a Frisbee
visit a museum

Unit 17

Technology
battery
calculator
computer
email address
gadget
internet
laptop
mobile phone
program
robot
smartphone
text (message)
video
web page
website

Verbs
be/go online
call
chat
check email
download
email
text
turn on

Verb + noun
get a bus
get a job
give a party
give someone a call
have a good time
have a job
have a party
have friends
make a film
make a noise
make friends
see a film
see friends
watch a film
watch TV

Unit 18

Parts of the body
arm
back
ear
eye
foot
hair
hand
head
leg
mouth
neck
nose

Health
ambulance
chemist
doctor
hospital
medicine
nurse
sick
temperature

Verb + noun
have a broken arm
  a cold
  a cut
  a headache
  a sore throat
  stomach ache
  toothache

Other verb phrases
be/feel sick
break a leg, arm, etc.
get better
get fit
go on a diet
go to sleep
have an accident
have a bad dream
hurt your arm
keep healthy
sleep well
wake up

Unit 19

Communication
email
envelope
Facebook
letter
mobile phone
note
phone message
postcard
stamp
telephone
text message

Languages
Arabic
Chinese
Cornish
Danish
Dutch
French
Gaelic
German
Greek
Italian
Japanese
Norwegian
Polish
Portuguese
Russian
Spanish

Swedish
Turkish
Welsh

Unit 20

Winning – nouns
competition
luck
prize

Adjectives
angry
awesome
broken
clever
famous
happy
kind
lucky
married
positive
single
special
worried

Practice for *Key* Writing Part 6

Unit 1
Read the descriptions of some adjectives about people and things.
What is the word for each one?
The first letter is already there. There is one space for each other letter in the word.

Example:
0 You can use this word to describe someone with lots of friends. p _ _ _ _ _ _

Answer: | 0 | popular |

1 This is what you are if you aren't busy and you are available to see friends. f _ _ _
2 If you are pleased about something, you feel this. h _ _ _ _
3 When something is not correct, it is this. w _ _ _ _
4 This is another way of saying someone is ill. s _ _ _
5 When something makes you laugh, it is this. f _ _ _ _

Unit 2
Read the descriptions of some things you can buy in a department store.
What is the word for each one?
The first letter is already there. There is one space for each other letter in the word.

Example:
0 When you wash your hands, you use some of this. s _ _ _

Answer: | 0 | soap |

1 You can take pictures of your friends with this. c _ _ _ _ _
2 Young children like playing with these. t _ _ _
3 You can wash your hair with this. s _ _ _ _ _ _
4 You hold this above your head when it is raining. u _ _ _ _ _ _ _
5 This has a picture on the front and may have a birthday message inside. c _ _ _

Unit 3
Read the descriptions of some things you can have for lunch.
What is the word for each one?
The first letter is already there. There is one space for each other letter in the word.

Example:
0 This is round and has cheese and tomatoes on it. p _ _ _ _

Answer: | 0 | pizza |

1 Oranges, apples and bananas are examples of this. f _ _ _ _
2 This usually has green vegetables in it and is very healthy. s _ _ _ _
3 You can have a slice of this sweet food for dessert. c _ _ _
4 This Italian food can be long or short and often comes with a tomato or meat sauce. p _ _ _ _
5 You eat this from a bowl with a spoon and it is good on a cold day. s _ _ _

Unit 4
Read the descriptions of some verbs.
What is the word for each one?
The first letter is already there. There is one space for each other letter in the word.

Example:
0 You use your ears to do this. l _ _ _ _ _ _

Answer: | 0 | listen |

1 This is what you do at the end of a journey when you get to a place. a _ _ _ _ _ _
2 You do this when you go or come back to a place. r _ _ _ _ _ _
3 When you hold something and take it somewhere else, you do this. c _ _ _ _
4 If you choose to do something, you do this. d _ _ _ _ _ _
5 This means to go to a place and spend some time there. v _ _ _ _

Unit 5

Read the descriptions of some animals.

What is the word for each one?

The first letter is already there. There is one space for each other letter in the word.

Example:
0 You can take this animal for a walk in the park. d _ _

Answer: | 0 | dog |

1 This is a large animal with four legs and you can ride it. h _ _ _ _
2 You can drink the milk of this large farm animal. c _ _
3 You can see this bird on rivers and lakes. d _ _ _
4 This very large animal is grey and has big ears. e _ _ _ _ _ _ _
5 This bird lives on a farm and its eggs are good to eat. c _ _ _ _ _ _

Unit 6

Read the descriptions of some adjectives to describe places and things.

What is the word for each one?

The first letter is already there. There is one space for each other letter in the word.

Example:
0 You can use this word to describe a mountain or a tall building. h _ _ _

Answer: | 0 | high |

1 Something that costs a lot of money is this. e _ _ _ _ _ _ _ _
2 This is a way of saying that something uses the newest ideas. m _ _ _ _ _
3 You can use this to describe something with a strong colour. b _ _ _ _ _
4 If a shop or a club is not open, it is this. c _ _ _ _ _
5 You can use this word to describe a beautiful place. a _ _ _ _ _ _ _ _ _

Unit 7

Read the descriptions of clothes or parts of clothes.

What is the word for each one?

The first letter is already there. There is one space for each other letter in the word.

Example:
0 You wear this on your head. h _ _

Answer: | 0 | hat |

1 This is a short coat that is sometimes made of leather. j _ _ _ _ _
2 You wear these on your feet inside your shoes. s _ _ _ _
3 Most coats have two of these for you to carry small things in. p _ _ _ _ _ _
4 If you buy a pair of these, make sure they are long enough for your legs. t _ _ _ _ _ _ _
5 This will keep the top half of your body warm in cold weather. s _ _ _ _ _ _

Unit 8

Read the descriptions of some things you might see at a music festival.

What is the word for each one?

The first letter is already there. There is one space for each other letter in the word.

Example:
0 This is a group of people playing rock music. b _ _ _

Answer: | 0 | band |

1 This instrument is round and you hit it to make a sound. d _ _ _
2 This instrument is often made of wood and is played with the hands. g _ _ _ _ _
3 You can buy this after a concert and listen to your favourite songs again. a _ _ _ _
4 When it gets dark, people turn these on so you can see the stage. l _ _ _ _ _
5 This large instrument makes different sounds when you play its black and white keyboard. p _ _ _ _

Unit 9

Read the descriptions of some things to take on holiday.

What is the word for each one?

The first letter is already there. There is one space for each other letter in the word.

Example:

0 You can wear these to look through on a bright day. s _ _ _ _ _ _ _ _ _

Answer: | 0 | sunglasses |

1 Suitcases and other kinds of bags are examples of this. l _ _ _ _ _ _
2 You need to show this when you arrive in another country. p _ _ _ _ _ _ _
3 This will give you lots of information about things to see in a place. g _ _ _ _ _ _ _ _
4 You need this to travel on a bus or a train. t _ _ _ _ _
5 This is a picture of all the roads and rivers in a city or area. m _ _

Unit 10

Read the descriptions of some things in a bedroom.

What is the word for each one?

The first letter is already there. There is one space for each other letter in the word.

Example:

0 You can put this on the wall to look at. p _ _ _ _ _

Answer: | 0 | poster |

1 This is a piece of glass and you can see yourself in it. m _ _ _ _ _
2 These are sometimes made of cotton and cover a window at night. c _ _ _ _ _ _ _
3 You need to use this when it is dark outside and you want to study. l _ _ _
4 This is soft and is under your head when you sleep. p _ _ _ _ _
5 You put this on the floor so your feet aren't cold. c _ _ _ _ _

Unit 11

Read the descriptions of some sports.

What is the word for each one?

The first letter is already there. There is one space for each other letter in the word.

Example:

0 This is a winter sport where you move quickly over snow with something on each foot. s _ _ _ _ _

Answer: | 0 | skiing |

1 You need a bat and a glove to play this American sport on a field. b _ _ _ _ _ _ _
2 In this sport, two teams of eleven players try to score goals during a 90-minute match. f _ _ _ _ _ _ _
3 You do this sport on the sea using a special board. s _ _ _ _ _ _
4 You can play this sport on the beach if there is a net. v _ _ _ _ _ _ _ _ _
5 Each player of this sport uses a racket to hit a ball over a net. t _ _ _ _ _

Unit 12

Read the descriptions of some family members.

What is the word for each one?

The first letter is already there. There is one space for each other letter in the word.

Example:

0 This is the word for someone's child if it is a girl. d _ _ _ _ _ _ _

Answer: | 0 | daughter |

1 This is the word for your father and mother. p _ _ _ _ _ _
2 This is the child of your aunt. c _ _ _ _ _
3 This man is married to your aunt. u _ _ _ _
4 This is your name for your mother or father's father. g _ _ _ _ _ _ _
5 This girl has the same mother and father as you. s _ _ _ _ _

PRACTICE FOR *KEY* WRITING PART 6

Unit 13

Read the descriptions of some weather words.
What is the word for each one?
The first letter is already there. There is one space for each other letter in the word.

Example:
0 In this weather, it is very difficult to see anything.
                                                        f _ _

Answer: | 0 | fog |

1 This is when the air moves very fast.   w _ _ _
2 People use umbrellas when this falls from dark clouds.   r _ _ _
3 This is soft and white, and falls from the sky in winter.   s _ _ _
4 You need to be careful if this is on the road during cold weather as it is dangerous.   i _ _
5 In this very bad weather you may hear thunder and it will be wet.   s _ _ _ _

Unit 14

Read the descriptions of school subjects.
What is the word for each one?
The first letter is already there. There is one space for each other letter in the word.

Example:
0 In this subject you paint or draw pictures.
                                                        a _ _

Answer: | 0 | art |

1 This subject is about the world and its seas, mountains and rivers.   g _ _ _ _ _ _ _ _
2 You need to understand numbers and add them together in this subject.   m _ _ _ _
3 In this subject you can study nature and find out how plants grow.   s _ _ _ _ _ _
4 For this subject, you learn dates and facts about what happened centuries ago.   h _ _ _ _ _ _
5 If you study this subject, you might be able to play an instrument.   m _ _ _ _

Unit 15

Read the descriptions of some jobs.
What is the word for each one?
The first letter is already there. There is one space for each other letter in the word.

Example:
0 This person repairs the engines of cars and buses.
                                                        m _ _ _ _ _ _ _

Answer: | 0 | mechanic |

1 This person works outside and often has animals such as cows or sheep.   f _ _ _ _ _
2 This person works in a hospital and helps sick people.   n _ _ _ _
3 This person brings food and drinks to customers in a restaurant.   w _ _ _ _ _
4 This person looks after your teeth.   d _ _ _ _ _ _
5 This person plans and cooks meals in a restaurant kitchen.   c _ _ _

Unit 16

Read the descriptions of things you can travel in.
What is the word for each one?
The first letter is already there. There is one space for each other letter in the word.

Example:
0 This has an engine, four wheels and seats for four or five people.   c _ _

Answer: | 0 | car |

1 A pilot flies this from one airport to another.   p _ _ _ _
2 This large boat carries people or things across the sea.   s _ _ _
3 You catch this at a station with lots of other people.   t _ _ _ _
4 This is a comfortable bus that can take groups of people on long journeys.   c _ _ _ _
5 This has two wheels but no engine.   b _ _ _ _ _

PRACTICE FOR *KEY* WRITING PART 6

Unit 17

Read the descriptions of computer things.

What is the word for each one?

The first letter is already there. There is one space for each other letter in the word.

Example:

0 You might need this to make your keyboard work and there is one in a mobile phone too.

b _ _ _ _ _ _

Answer: | 0 | battery |

1 You can watch lots of these on the internet.
v _ _ _ _ _
2 This gives information about something and is read online. w _ _ _ _ _ _
3 This is a message you send from your computer.
e _ _ _ _
4 You can carry this small computer around with you easily. l _ _ _ _ _
5 This is the instructions that make a computer do something. p _ _ _ _ _ _

Unit 18

Read the descriptions of things about health.

What is the word for each one?

The first letter is already there. There is one space for each other letter in the word.

Example:

0 Sick people are driven to hospital quickly in this.
a _ _ _ _ _ _ _ _

Answer: | 0 | ambulance |

1 If you are ill, you may need to take this to feel better. m _ _ _ _ _ _ _
2 This person finds out what is wrong with you and decides how to help you get better.
d _ _ _ _ _
3 A nurse takes this to find out how hot or cold your body is. t _ _ _ _ _ _ _ _ _ _
4 At this shop you can buy things to make you better. c _ _ _ _ _ _
5 If you have this, you should go to a dentist immediately. t _ _ _ _ _ _ _ _

Unit 19

Read the descriptions of different ways of contacting people.

What is the word for each one?

The first letter is already there. There is one space for each other letter in the word.

Example:

0 This is a phone that you have with you all the time. m _ _ _ _ _

Answer: | 0 | mobile |

1 You put a letter inside this when you post it.
e _ _ _ _ _ _ _
2 If you want to leave a message on your friend's desk, you may write this. n _ _ _
3 You buy this to put on a letter that you want to send by post. s _ _ _ _
4 This has a picture on one side and you can send it to your family from another place.
p _ _ _ _ _ _ _
5 You receive this type of message on your phone.
t _ _ _

Unit 20

Read the descriptions of some adjectives about people.

What is the word for each one?

The first letter is already there. There is one space for each other letter in the word.

Example:

0 If you are this, good things often happen to you.
l _ _ _ _

Answer: | 0 | lucky |

1 This describes a person who is not married.
s _ _ _ _ _
2 A big movie star or a popular singer will be this.
f _ _ _ _ _
3 Someone who helps you a lot when you have problems is this. k _ _ _
4 If you think someone's clothes are amazing, you might describe them as this. a _ _ _ _ _ _
5 Someone with problems may feel like this.
w _ _ _ _ _ _

PRACTICE FOR *KEY* WRITING PART 6

Irregular verbs

Here is a list of the irregular verbs you need to know at A2 level.

Infinitive	Past simple	Past participle	Infinitive	Past simple	Past participle
be	was/were	been	mean	meant	meant
become	became	become	meet	met	met
begin	began	begun	pay	paid	paid
break	broke	broken	put	put	put
bring	brought	brought	read	read	read
build	built	built	ride	rode	ridden
burn	burnt/burned	burnt/burned	ring	rang	rung
buy	bought	bought	run	ran	run
catch	caught	caught	say	said	said
choose	chose	chosen	see	saw	seen
come	came	come	sell	sold	sold
cost	cost	cost	send	sent	sent
cut	cut	cut	show	showed	shown
do	did	done	shut	shut	shut
draw	drew	drawn	sing	sang	sung
dream	dreamt/dreamed	dreamt/dreamed	sit	sat	sat
drink	drank	drunk	sleep	slept	slept
drive	drove	driven	speak	spoke	spoken
eat	ate	eaten	spell	spelt/spelled	spelt/spelled
fall	fell	fallen	spend	spent	spent
feel	felt	felt	stand	stood	stood
find	found	found	steal	stole	stolen
fly	flew	flown	swim	swam	swum
forget	forgot	forgotten	take	took	taken
get	got	got	teach	taught	taught
give	gave	given	tell	told	told
go	went	gone/been	think	thought	thought
grow	grew	grown	throw	threw	thrown
have	had	had	understand	understood	understood
hear	heard	heard	wake	woke	woken
hit	hit	hit	wear	wore	worn
hold	held	held	win	won	won
hurt	hurt	hurt	write	wrote	written
keep	kept	kept			
know	knew	known			
learn	learnt/learned	learnt/learned			
leave	left	left			
lend	lent	lent			
lie	lay	lain			
lose	lost	lost			
make	made	made			

Acknowledgements

Thanks and Acknowledgements

The authors would like to give their warmest thanks to Alyson Maskell for her many useful suggestions on both editions and her meticulous attention to detail, to Lynn Townsend at Cambridge University Press for her steadfast support and practical help on the second edition, and to Sue Ashcroft for her original editorial input on the first edition. Thanks also go to Stephanie White at Kamae for her creative design solutions.

The authors and publishers would like to thank the teachers who commented on the material for the new edition in the development stage: Andrew Cook, Anna Goy and Jessica Smith, and Annie Broadhead for her comments on the Exam folders.

Development of this publication has made use of the Cambridge English Corpus (CEC). the CEC is a computer database of contemporary spoken and written English, which currently stands at over one billion words. It includes British English, American English and other varieties of English. It also includes the Cambridge Learner Corpus, developed in collaboration with the University of Cambridge ESOL Examinations. Cambridge University Press has built up the CEC to provide evidence about language use that helps to produce better language teaching materials.

This product is informed by the English Vocabulary Profile, developed as part of English Profile, a collaborative programme designed to enhance the learning, teaching and assessment of English worldwide. Its main funding partners are Cambridge University Press and Cambridge ESOL and its aim is to create 'reference level descriptions' for English linked to the Common European Framework (CEF). English Profile outcomes, such as the English Vocabulary Profile, will provide detailed information about the language that learners can be expected to demonstrate at each CEF level, offering a clear benchmark for learners' proficiency. For more information, please visit www.englishprofile.org

The authors and publishers acknowledge the following sources of copyright material and are grateful for the permissions granted. While every effort has been made, it has not always been possible to identify the sources of all the material used, or to trace all copyright holders. If any omissions are brought to our notice, we will be happy to include the appropriate acknowledgements on reprinting.

Guardian News & Media Ltd for the text on p. 69 adapted from 'Q&A: Eniola Aluko', www.guardian.co.uk 24.05.10. Copyright © Guardian News & Media Ltd 2010; Cambridge University Press for the questionnaire on p. 130 from Activity Box by Joan Greenwood, 1997. Copyright © Cambridge University Press. Reprinted with permission of Cambridge University Press and Joan Greenwood.

The authors and publishers acknowledge the following sources of copyright material and are grateful for the permissions granted. While every effort has been made, it has not always been possible to identify the sources of all the material used, or to trace all copyright holders. If any omissions are brought to our notice, we will be happy to include the appropriate acknowledgements on reprinting.

T = Top, C = Centre, B = Below, L = Left, R = Right, U = Upper, Lo = Lower, B/G = background

p. 8 (TL): Getty Images/Stone/James Darell; p. 8 (CL): Getty Images/Taxi/Antonio Mo; p. 8 (CR): Thinkstock/Photodisc; p. 8 (BL): Thinkstock/Comstock; p. 8 (BR): Superstock/© SOMOS; p. 9 (TR, TL): Thinkstock/Photodisc; p. 9 (CR, BR): Thinkstock/Digital Vision; p. 9 (BL): Thinkstock/iStockphoto; p. 22: Steve Davcy; p. 23 (L): Corbis/Nordicphotos/ © Bertil Hertzberg; p. 23 (R): Thinkstock/iStockphoto; p. 26 (TL): Shutterstock/Jose Ignacio Soto; p. 26 (TR): Getty Images/LOCOG; p. 26 (TC): Getty Images/AFP/YOSHIKAZU TSUNO; p. 26 (B): Photo: "Skookum Jim" – James Mason, 1898. Source: Library and Archives Canada/International Harvester Company of Canada collection/C-025640; p. 28 (T): Getty Images/Taxi/Lisa Peardon; p. 28 (UC): Corbis/©Robert Holmes; p. 28 (LoC): Corbis/©Ed Kash; p. 28 (B): Corbis/©Jose Fuste Raga; p. 31 (BL): Corbis/© Phil Schermeister; p. 31 (R): Topfoto.co.uk/POLFOTO/ Thomas Borberg; p. 32 (TL, TC, BCR, BR): Thinkstock/iStockphoto; p. 32 (TR): Thinkstock/F1online; p. 32 (CR): Shutterstock/Micimakin; p. 32 (CL): Shutterstock/meunierd; p. 32 (BCL): Shutterstock/Peter Wey; p. 34: Getty Images/Stone/Daniel J Cox; p. 35: Rex Features/James D. Morgan; p. 37: Getty Images/Taxi/Gail Shumway; p. 38 (TL): Shutterstock/Racheal Grazias; p. 38 (TC): Rex Features/Sipa Press; p. 38 (TR): Thinkstock/Hemera; p. 39: ©Ferrari World Abu Dhabi www.ferrariworldabudhabi.com; p. 40: Thinkstock/iStockphoto; p. 43: Thinkstock/Hemera; p. 44 (L): Shutterstock/EML; p. 44 (C): iStockphoto/Kubrak78; p. 44 (R): Shutterstock/Neveshkin Nikolay; p. 48: Corbis/© Jean-Pierre Lescourret; p. 50 (TR): Twentieth Century-Fox Film Corporation/The Kobal Collection; p. 50 (CL): Walt Disney Pictures/The Kobal Collection; p. 50 (BL): Columbia/Paramount/Wingnut/Amblin/The Kobal Collection; p. 50 (B/G): Alamy/© M.Brodie; p. 51: Paramount Pictures/ The Kobal Collection; p. 52: Getty Images/Samir Hussein; p. 53: Rex Features/Picture Perfect; p. 54: Walt Disney Pictures/The Kobal Collection; p. 55: Rex Features/©SIPA Press; p. 56 (BR): Corbis/© Ocean; p. 56 (BL, TL): Thinkstock/iStockphoto; p. 56 (TR): Getty Images/Taxi/David Nardini; p. 64 (TCL): Superstock/© Hemis.fr; p. 64 (L): SuperStock/Flirt; p. 64 (BR): Rex Features/Action Press/Uwe Gerig; p. 64 (BCL, TR): Thinkstock/iStockphoto; p. 64 (CR): Shutterstock/Steve Rosset; p. 65: Shutterstock/Zsolt, Biczó; p. 67 (T): Alamy/© Jason O. Watson; p. 67 (B): Alamy/© Robert Martin; p. 68 (TL): Rex Features; p. 68 (TR): Shutterstock/Nurlan Kalchinov; p. 68 (TC): Thinkstock/Hemera; p. 68 (B): Rex Features/SIPA/Chine Nouvelle; p. 68 (BC): Thinkstock/Brand X Pictures; p. 68 (BR): Getty Images/Cameron Spencer; p. 69: Alamy/Diadem Images /© Jonathan Larsen; p. 74: Getty Images/WireImage/Steve Granitz; p. 76: ©Bernice Hayden; p. 80 (L): Getty Images/Photographer's Choice/Frank Cezus; p. 80 (TCL, BCR): Thinkstock/iStockphoto; p. 80 (BCL): Getty Images/Stone/Ralph Wetmore; p. 80 (TCR): Getty Images/Taxi/Getty Images; p. 80 (TR): Getty Images/Riser/Color Day Production; p. 80 (BR): Corbis/Reuters/©Richard Chung; p. 83: ©Warren Faidley/Stormchaser; p. 86 (R): Thinkstock/Photos.com; p. 86 (TL): Thinkstock/Photodisc; p. 86 (BL): Thinkstock/Image Source; p. 88: Getty Images/Stone/Dale Durfee; p. 92 (TL): ©Bubbles/Jennie Woodcock; p. 92 (TC): Shutterstock/Mircea Bezergheanu; p. 92 (TR): ©2002Topham/PA/Topfoto.co.uk; p. 92 (BL): Shutterstock/Igor Bulgarin; p. 92 (BR): Getty Images/The Image Bank/James Schnepf; p. 94 (L): ©Bubbles; p. 94 (C): Thinkstock/Brand X Pictures; p. 94 (R): Thinkstock/iStockphoto; p. 95: Alamy/© Andrew Michael; p. 102: Getty Images/Taxi/Angela Scott; p. 105 (C): Getty Images/Stone/Javier Pierini; p. 105 (L): Science Museum / SSPL; p. 105 (R): Alamy/© Christopher Stewart; p. 106 (BR): Rex Features/Zuma/KPA; p. 106 (TR): Rex Features/Jonathan Hordle; p. 106 (C): Getty Images/The Image Bank/Geir Pettersen; p. 106 (R): Rex Features/Marja Airio; p. 110 (a, h, j): Getty Images/Taxi; p. 110 (b, c, e, g, i, k): Superstock/© PhotoAlto; p. 110 (d, f, l): Getty Images/Riser/Sean Justice; p. 112 (T): Topfoto/©2006 Alinari; p. 112 (C): Getty Images/AFP; p. 112 (B): Getty Images/AFP/Oscar Pipkin; p. 115: Corbis/©Robert Garvey; p. 124 (L): Rex Features/Aflo; p. 124 (R): Getty Images/Carlos Alvarez; p. 124 (C), 125: Rex Features; p. 128: Thinkstock/F1online.

Commissioned photography by: Gareth Boden pp. 10, 21, 60.

Illustrations by: James Brown, Kai Chan, Mark Duffin, Joanna Kerr, Francis Fung, Paul Howalt, Janos Jantner, Javier Joaquin, Inigo Montoya, Julian Mosedale, Andrew Painter, David Whittle

Photo research by Hilary Fletcher

Cover concept by Tim Elcock

Produced by Kamae Design, Oxford